Better Homes and Gardens®

Indoor
GRILLING

Kath
Happy Birthday '03
Dad

Better Homes and Gardens® Books
Des Moines, Iowa

All of us at Better Homes and Gardens® Books are dedicated to providing you with the information and ideas you need to create delicious foods. We welcome your comments and suggestions. Write to us at Better Homes and Gardens Books, Cookbook Editorial Department, 1716 Locust St., Des Moines, IA 50309-3023.

If you would like to purchase any of our books, check wherever quality books are sold. Visit our website at bhg.com.

Our seal assures you that every recipe in *Indoor Grilling* has been tested in the Better Homes and Gardens® Test Kitchen. This means that each recipe is practical and reliable, and meets our high standards of taste appeal. We guarantee your satisfaction with this book for as long as you own it.

Printed in China. First Edition—00
Library of Congress Catalog Card Number: 00-133307
ISBN: 0-696-21238-2

Pictured on front cover: Jamaican Chops with Melon Salsa, page 35

Cover Photo: Andy Lyons, Photographer; Dianna Nolin, Food Stylist

Better Homes and Gardens® Books
An imprint of Meredith® Books

Indoor Grilling

Editor: Jennifer Dorland Darling
Contributing Editor: Spectrum Communication Services, Inc.
Associate Art Director: Lynda Haupert
Copy Chief: Catherine Hamrick
Copy and Production Editor: Terri Fredrickson
Managers, Book Production: Pam Kvitne, Marjorie J. Schenkelberg
Contributing Copy Editor: Kim Catanzarite
Contributing Proofreaders: Gretchen Kauffman, Susan J. Kling, Debra Morris Smith
Electronic Production Coordinator: Paula Forest
Editorial and Design Assistants: Judy Bailey, Mary Lee Gavin, Karen Schirm
Test Kitchen Director: Lynn Blanchard
Test Kitchen Product Supervisor: Marilyn Cornelius
Test Kitchen Home Economists: Patricia Beebout, Judy Comstock, Maryellyn Krantz, Tammy Leonard, Jan Miller, R.D., Jill Moberly, Jennifer Peterson, Kay Springer, Colleen Weeden, Lori Wilson, Charles Worthington

Meredith® Books

Editor in Chief: James D. Blume
Design Director: Matt Strelecki
Managing Editor: Gregory H. Kayko

Director, Retail Sales and Marketing: Terry Unsworth
Director, Sales, Special Markets: Rita McMullen
Director, Sales, Premiums: Michael A. Peterson
Director, Sales, Retail: Tom Wierzbicki
Director, Sales, Home & Garden Centers: Ray Wolf
Director, Book Marketing: Brad Elmitt
Director, Operations: George A. Susral
Director, Production: Douglas M. Johnston

Vice President, General Manager: Jamie L. Martin

Better Homes and Gardens® Magazine

Editor in Chief: Jean LemMon
Executive Food Editor: Nancy Byal

Meredith Publishing Group

President, Publishing Group: Christopher M. Little
Vice President, Finance & Administration: Max Runciman

Meredith Corporation

Chairman and Chief Executive Officer: William T. Kerr

Chairman of the Executive Committee: E. T. Meredith III

Contents

Welcome to Our Kitchen

When you cook with a Better Homes and Gardens® cookbook, you can be confident that every recipe will taste great every time. That's because we perfect every recipe in our Test Kitchen before we present it to you.

Occasionally a versatile appliance comes along that has lasting impact because it makes life easier and produces delicious results. We think indoor electric grills are just such an innovation.

Intrigued by the convenience and simplicity of indoor grills, we put our vast experience with outdoor grilling to use in compiling these recipes. And with Better Homes and Gardens, you're guaranteed that every recipe chosen is a superstar in the taste category!

Throughout recipe testing we kept detailed notes so we could pass along helpful advice on everything from grill safety to grilling veggies to speedy cleanup. (Look for these tips on pages 12, 72, and 79, along with our Secrets to Success on page 5.) If you're looking for low-fat recipes, look for ♥. This symbol identifies main-dish recipes with 10 grams or less of total fat.

To ensure your grilling success, we tested the recipes on a variety of indoor grills, including West Bend, Hamilton Beach, George Foreman, T-Fal, and Rival. You can be confident that the recipes will work for your grill.

Trying new recipes and finding ways to make them convenient for you—and always maintaining great taste—is a personal and professional pleasure. We hope you and your family have a great time sampling these full-of-flavor foods hot off your indoor grill.

Lynn Blanchard

Lynn Blanchard
Better Homes and Gardens®
Test Kitchen Director

Secrets to Success

Need help with your indoor grill? Rely on the Home Economists in the Better Homes and Gardens® Test Kitchen. Because they've used indoor grills extensively, they know the best techniques for indoor grilling. Here are the answers to some of the most-asked questions.

Q.

I've noticed that indoor grills come in many styles and sizes. Will the directions in this book work for all types?

A.

Despite the many styles and sizes, there are *only* two types of indoor grills: covered and uncovered. Covered grills typically have a hinged lid, and foods are cooked with the lid closed. Because foods are heated from both the top and bottom, they cook more quickly than they would on an uncovered grill. Uncovered grills are open, and foods are heated from the bottom only, so foods cook more slowly than on a covered grill. Grills that are sold as part of ranges with special grates and exhaust fans also fit into this category. The recipes in this book will work for both types of grills. Simply follow the directions and timings for a covered or an uncovered grill according to your appliance. Your grill may take a bit more or less time to cook, so use the timings as guidelines. If your grill has different temperature settings, check the manufacturer's directions to determine the recommended setting for the food you're grilling.

Q.

What foods can I grill on my indoor grill?

A.

Indoor electric grills can be used for the direct grilling of foods only up to 1 inch thick. Burgers; skinless, boneless chicken breasts; turkey tenderloin steaks; fish fillets and steaks; hot dogs; bratwurst; steaks; chops; and grilled sandwiches all work well.

For covered grills, boneless cuts of meat work best. The bones in steaks or chops may prevent the lid from closing completely and may cause uneven cooking. If a recipe in this book calls for a bone-in cut, simply substitute a boneless cut as suggested.

Q.

Do I need to grease the grill rack?

A.

Because most indoor grills have grill racks with nonstick surfaces, you should not need to grease the rack unless you're cooking poultry, fish, seafood, or vegetables. For these foods, lightly brush cooking oil over the rack, or lightly coat the rack with nonstick cooking spray before preheating. To protect the nonstick surface of the grill rack, use only plastic or wooden utensils so you don't scratch the surface. When the food is cooked, transfer it to a plate or cutting board before cutting it into serving-size portions.

Q.

Should I turn foods during grilling?

A.

When using a covered indoor grill, you don't need to turn most foods because they cook and brown from both the top and bottom at the same time. For kabobs, however, it helps to give the skewers a quarter turn once halfway through grilling to ensure the cubes of meat and pieces of vegetables cook evenly.

When cooking on an uncovered grill, turn serving-size pieces once halfway through grilling. Turn kabobs occasionally during grilling.

Q.

Can I baste foods with sauces?

A.

When cooking on a covered grill, we suggest you brush most sauces on foods the last 1 to 2 minutes of grilling.

If you're using an uncovered grill, brush the foods after they've been turned halfway through grilling. For best results when using sweet or tomato-based sauces, brush them on only during the last 5 minutes of grilling to prevent excessive browning and burning.

Small Grill Savvy

My grill isn't big enough to cook all the food in many recipes. What can I do?

When selecting a recipe in this book, look for the SMALL GRILL symbol at the top of the page. It tells you the recipe works well for a small grill because it is scaled to make 2 servings. In addition, consider one of the following:

● If not all of the meat will fit on your grill, cook it in batches. Remove the first batch and cover it to keep it warm while grilling the second batch. If a recipe calls for grilling meat and vegetables at the same time, grill the meat first, then the veggies.

● Choose recipes that can be halved easily. Generally these recipes call for serving-size pieces of meat and have a sauce, marinade, or salsa which can be halved without worrying about precise measurements.

● If a recipe can't be easily halved, use only half of the meat in a recipe, but make the entire amount of sauce, marinade, or salsa. Before you begin cooking, store half of the sauce for use with another meal.

Steaks

Argentinean-Style Steak

In this Chapter:

Jalapeño-Glazed Rib Eyes

Using jalapeño pepper jelly, whip up a quick, spicy-sweet glaze that adds sizzle to these steaks. The pepper jelly also lends a kick to the corn relish (add a jalapeño for real warmth).

Prep: 20 minutes **Grill:** 4 minutes (covered) or 8 minutes (uncovered) **Serves:** 4

Glaze

- ¼ cup jalapeño pepper jelly
- ¼ cup catsup

- 4 boneless beef rib eye steaks, cut 1 inch thick (1¾ to 2 pounds total)

Relish

- 2 tablespoons jalapeño pepper jelly
- 1 tablespoon lime juice
- ½ teaspoon chili powder
- ¼ teaspoon ground cumin
- 1 10-ounce package frozen whole kernel corn, thawed
- ¾ cup chopped red sweet pepper
- ¼ cup finely chopped green onions
- 1 fresh jalapeño pepper, seeded and finely chopped (optional)

- Green onions (optional)

1 Preheat indoor electric grill. For glaze, in a small saucepan melt the ¼ cup jelly. Stir in catsup; set aside.

2 Trim fat from steaks. Place steaks on the grill rack. If using a covered grill, close lid. Grill until steaks are desired doneness. (For a covered grill, allow 4 to 6 minutes for medium rare or 6 to 8 minutes for medium, brushing once with glaze the last 1 to 2 minutes of grilling. For an uncovered grill, allow 8 to 12 minutes for medium rare or 12 to 15 minutes for medium, turning once halfway through and brushing occasionally with glaze the last half of grilling.)

3 Meanwhile, for relish, in another small saucepan stir together the 2 tablespoons jelly, the lime juice, chili powder, and cumin. Cook and stir until jelly is melted and mixture is bubbly. Stir in corn, sweet pepper, chopped green onions, and, if desired, jalapeño pepper. Cook and stir just until heated through. Season to taste with salt. Serve the steaks with relish. If desired, garnish with additional green onions.

Nutrition Facts per serving: 680 cal., 41 g total fat (16 g sat. fat), 131 mg chol., 290 mg sodium, 42 g carbo., 3 g fiber, 38 g pro.
Daily Values: 18% vit. A, 89% vit. C, 4% calcium, 24% iron

Steak Caribbean

Yes, we have grilled bananas—and black beans and rice to complement coriander-cumin-rubbed steaks. One bite will take you to a dreamy climate where the lime tree grows.

Prep: 25 minutes **Grill:** 8 minutes (covered) or 14 minutes (uncovered) **Serves:** 4

4 boneless beef rib eye steaks, cut 1 inch thick (1¾ to 2 pounds total)
4 cloves garlic, minced
1½ teaspoons ground cumin
1 teaspoon ground coriander
¼ teaspoon salt
⅛ to ¼ teaspoon ground red pepper
2 tablespoons lime juice
1 teaspoon finely shredded orange peel
1 teaspoon margarine or butter, melted
2 large firm bananas or fully ripe plantains,* peeled and cut in half lengthwise and crosswise
⅔ cup uncooked long-grain rice
½ cup cooked or canned black beans, rinsed and drained
2 tablespoons finely chopped red sweet pepper

1 Trim fat from steaks. Combine garlic, cumin, coriander, salt, and ground red pepper. Reserve ¼ teaspoon spice mixture for rice. Brush both sides of steaks with 1 tablespoon of the lime juice. Sprinkle the remaining spice mixture evenly over steaks; rub in with your fingers. Combine the remaining 1 tablespoon lime juice, the orange peel, and melted margarine. Brush on both sides of bananas. Set aside.

2 Preheat indoor electric grill. Cook the rice in lightly salted water according to package directions, except add the reserved spice mixture to cooking liquid. Stir beans and sweet pepper into cooked rice; heat through.

3 Meanwhile, place steaks on the grill rack. If using a covered grill, close lid. Grill until steaks are desired doneness. (For a covered grill, allow 4 to 6 minutes for medium rare or 6 to 8 minutes for medium. For an uncovered grill, allow 8 to 12 minutes for medium rare or 12 to 15 minutes for medium, turning once halfway through grilling.) Remove from grill; cover and keep warm.

4 Add bananas to the grill rack. If using a covered grill, close lid. Grill until bananas are heated through. (For a covered grill, allow 4 to 5 minutes. For an uncovered grill, allow 6 to 7 minutes, turning once halfway through grilling.) Serve steaks with bananas and rice mixture.

Nutrition Facts per serving: 417 cal., 13 g total fat (5 g sat. fat), 67 mg chol., 214 mg sodium, 46 g carbo., 2 g fiber, 28 g pro.
Daily Values: 5% vit. A, 24% vit. C, 4% calcium, 35% iron

*Note: Fully ripe plantains are still slightly firm, but have skin that has turned mostly black. If the plantains are not fully ripe, cook them a few minutes longer than directed above.

Garlic Steaks with Nectarine Relish ♥

In the summertime, there's nothing better than a juicy steak on the grill. Serve this garlic-stuffed beef with some crusty bread to soak up the delicious juices.

Prep: 15 minutes **Marinate:** 20 minutes **Grill:** 4 minutes (covered) or 8 minutes (uncovered) **Serves:** 4

4 boneless beef top loin steaks, cut 1 inch thick (1¾ to 2 pounds total)

6 cloves garlic, thinly sliced

Relish

2 medium onions, coarsely chopped

1 teaspoon olive oil

2 tablespoons cider vinegar

1 tablespoon honey

1 medium nectarine, chopped

2 teaspoons snipped fresh applemint, pineapplemint, or mint

Fresh applemint, pineapplemint, or mint sprigs (optional)

1 Trim fat from steaks. With the tip of a paring knife, make small slits in steaks; insert half of the garlic into slits. Wrap steaks in plastic wrap; let stand at room temperature up to 20 minutes. Sprinkle with salt and pepper.

2 Meanwhile, for relish, in a large nonstick skillet cook onions and remaining garlic in hot olive oil over medium heat about 5 minutes or until onions are golden, stirring occasionally. Stir in vinegar and honey. Stir in nectarine and the snipped mint; heat through.

3 Preheat indoor electric grill. Place steaks on the grill rack. If using a covered grill, close lid. Grill until steaks are desired doneness. (For a covered grill, allow 4 to 6 minutes for medium rare or 6 to 8 minutes for medium. For an uncovered grill, allow 8 to 12 minutes for medium rare or 12 to 15 minutes for medium, turning once halfway through grilling.) Serve the steaks with relish. If desired, garnish with mint sprigs.

Nutrition Facts per serving: 272 cal., 9 g total fat (3 g sat. fat), 97 mg chol., 108 mg sodium, 13 g carbo., 1 g fiber, 34 g pro.
Daily Values: 2% vit. A, 9% vit. C, 2% calcium, 27% iron

Steaks with Tomato-Garlic Butter

Beef steaks take kindly to the enhancement of butter, especially this tangy, garlic-infused blend. Simply double the butter recipe, and you'll have enough to spread on warm bread.

Prep: 12 minutes **Grill:** 4 minutes (covered) or 8 minutes (uncovered) **Serves:** 4

Butter

- ½ cup butter, softened
- 1 tablespoon snipped oil-packed dried tomatoes
- 1 tablespoon chopped kalamata olives
- 1 tablespoon finely chopped green onion
- 1 clove garlic, minced

- 4 boneless beef top loin steaks, cut 1 inch thick (1¾ to 2 pounds total)

1 Preheat indoor electric grill. For butter, in a small bowl stir together softened butter, dried tomatoes, kalamata olives, green onion, and garlic. Set aside.

2 Trim fat from steaks. Place steaks on the grill rack. If using a covered grill, close lid. Grill until steaks are desired doneness. (For a covered grill, allow 4 to 6 minutes for medium rare or 6 to 8 minutes for medium. For an uncovered grill, allow 8 to 12 minutes for medium rare or 12 to 15 minutes for medium, turning once halfway through grilling.)

3 If desired, sprinkle steaks with salt and pepper. Spread 1 tablespoon of the butter over each steak. Cover and refrigerate the remaining butter for another time.

Nutrition Facts per serving: 383 cal., 22 g total fat (11 g sat. fat), 161 mg chol., 227 mg sodium, 0 g carbo., 0 g fiber, 45 g pro.
Daily Values: 10% vit. A, 1% vit. C, 1% calcium, 32% iron

safety first!

Open the box and pull out your new indoor grill. Although you're probably anxious to get grilling, take a few minutes to review these indoor grilling rules of the road:

- Always use an indoor electric grill on a dry, level, heatproof surface. (Placing the grill on the range under the exhaust fan will help expel cooking odors.)

- Don't use the grill outdoors unless it is designed for both indoor and outdoor use.

- Tuck the grill cord out of the way so it doesn't touch the hot grill or hang over the counter.

- Unplug the grill when you're not using it and before you clean it.

- Don't immerse the grill in water unless the manufacturer's directions specify to do so. Never immerse the cord, plug, or heat control in water.

Argentinean-Style Steak SMALL GRILL

In Argentina, one steak house specialty is a quick sauce flavored with Italian parsley and oregano. It's a perfect way to give an already-grand piece of grilled beef a final zap of flavor.

Prep: 10 minutes **Grill:** 8 minutes (uncovered) **Serves:** 2

Sauce

1 tablespoon snipped fresh Italian flat-leaf parsley
1 tablespoon olive oil
1½ teaspoons snipped fresh oregano or ½ teaspoon dried oregano, crushed
1 clove garlic, minced
⅛ teaspoon salt
⅛ teaspoon ground red pepper

1 beef T-bone or porterhouse steak,* cut 1 inch thick (about 1 pound)

1 Preheat *uncovered* indoor electric grill. For sauce, in a small bowl stir together the parsley, olive oil, oregano, garlic, salt, and red pepper.

2 Trim fat from steak. Place steak on the grill rack. Grill until steak is desired doneness. (Allow 8 to 12 minutes for medium rare or 12 to 15 minutes for medium, turning once halfway through and spooning sauce over steak the last 2 minutes of grilling.) Cut steak in half.

Nutrition Facts per serving: 574 cal., 43 g total fat (15 g sat. fat), 137 mg chol., 249 mg sodium, 1 g carbo., 0 g fiber, 43 g pro.
Daily Values: 2% vit. A, 5% vit. C, 2% calcium, 26% iron

*Note: If you have a covered grill, substitute 2 boneless beef top loin or rib eye steaks, cut 1 inch thick (about 1 pound total), for the T-bone or porterhouse steak. Preheat grill. Place steaks on the grill rack; close lid. Grill until desired doneness. (Allow 4 to 6 minutes for medium rare or 6 to 8 minutes for medium, spooning sauce over steaks the last 2 minutes of grilling.)

Soy Flank Steak

A bold marinade made with soy sauce, fresh ginger, rice vinegar, and sesame oil gets their attention. The tangy Chinese-cabbage-and-carrot slaw adds a crisp, refreshing complement.

Prep: 20 minutes **Marinate:** 2 hours **Grill:** 7 minutes (covered) or 12 minutes (uncovered) **Serves:** 6

Dressing
- 3 tablespoons rice vinegar
- 2 tablespoons sesame seed, toasted
- 2 tablespoons thinly sliced green onion
- 2 tablespoons reduced-sodium soy sauce
- 2 tablespoons grated fresh ginger
- 2 teaspoons brown sugar
- ⅓ cup peanut oil
- 1 tablespoon toasted sesame oil

- 1 1¼-pound beef flank steak

Slaw
- 6 cups shredded Chinese cabbage
- 1 cup coarsely shredded carrots
- 2 tablespoons snipped fresh cilantro

1 For dressing, in a medium bowl combine vinegar, sesame seed, green onion, soy sauce, ginger, and brown sugar; stir until sugar dissolves. Slowly whisk in peanut oil and sesame oil.

2 Trim fat from steak. Score steak by making shallow diagonal cuts at 1-inch intervals in a diamond pattern. Repeat on other side. Place steak in a plastic bag set in a shallow dish. Pour half of the dressing over steak; seal bag. Marinate in the refrigerator for 2 hours, turning bag occasionally.

3 Meanwhile, for slaw, combine cabbage, carrots, cilantro, and the remaining dressing; toss to coat. Cover and refrigerate until ready to serve.

4 Preheat indoor electric grill. Drain steak, discarding marinade. Place steak on the grill rack. If using a covered grill, close lid. Grill until steak is desired doneness. (For a covered grill, allow 7 to 9 minutes for medium. For an uncovered grill, allow 12 to 14 minutes for medium, turning once halfway through grilling.) Thinly slice steak diagonally across the grain. Serve with slaw.

Nutrition Facts per serving: 292 cal., 20 g total fat (5 g sat. fat), 44 mg chol., 217 mg sodium, 9 g carbo., 2 g fiber, 20 g pro.
Daily Values: 61% vit. A, 37% vit. C, 6% calcium, 16% iron

tenderizing flank steak

Flank steak is one of my favorite steaks for grilling. Unless you tenderize it by scoring or marinating, though, you're in for some real tug-of-war when you bite into it. To make sure it's tender, cut it diagonally across the grain into very thin slices for serving.

Lori Wilson
Test Kitchen Home Economist

Herb-Pepper Sirloin Steak ♥

A robust mixture of catsup, fresh herbs, and pepper coats both sides of this sirloin steak, accenting the hearty beef flavor. Grilled sweet peppers round out the meal handsomely.

Prep: 10 minutes **Grill:** 5 minutes (covered) or 12 minutes (uncovered) **Serves:** 4

1 tablespoon catsup
1 teaspoon snipped fresh
    rosemary or ¼ teaspoon
    dried rosemary, crushed
1 teaspoon snipped fresh
    basil or ¼ teaspoon
    dried basil, crushed
¼ teaspoon coarsely ground
    pepper
    Dash garlic powder
    Dash ground cardamom
    (optional)
1 1-pound boneless beef
    sirloin steak, cut 1 inch
    thick
    Fresh rosemary sprigs
    (optional)

1 Preheat indoor electric grill. In a small bowl stir together catsup, the snipped fresh or dried rosemary, basil, pepper, garlic powder, and, if desired, cardamom. Trim fat from steak. Coat both sides of steak with catsup mixture.

2 Place steak on the grill rack. If using a covered grill, close lid. Grill until steak is desired doneness. (For a covered grill, allow 5 to 7 minutes for medium rare or 7 to 9 minutes for medium. For an uncovered grill, allow 12 to 15 minutes for medium rare or 15 to 18 minutes for medium, turning once halfway through grilling.) Cut into serving-size pieces. If desired, garnish with rosemary sprigs.

Nutrition Facts per
serving: 144 cal.,
4 g total fat
(1 g sat. fat),
53 mg chol.,
105 mg sodium,
1 g carbo., 0 g fiber,
24 g pro.
Daily Values:
1% vit. A, 1% vit. C,
2% calcium, 14% iron

Beef with Cucumber Raita ♥

The oft-fiery cuisine of India offers a respite in the form of a raita, a simple, cooling salad made with yogurt and fruits or vegetables. Mint makes this raita particularly flavorful and refreshing.

Prep: 15 minutes   **Grill:** 5 minutes (covered) or 12 minutes (uncovered)   **Serves:** 4

Raita

- 1 8-ounce carton plain fat-free or low-fat yogurt
- ¼ cup coarsely shredded unpeeled cucumber
- 1 tablespoon finely chopped red or yellow onion
- 1 tablespoon snipped fresh mint
- ¼ teaspoon sugar

- 1 pound boneless beef sirloin steak, cut 1 inch thick
- ½ teaspoon lemon-pepper seasoning
  Fresh mint leaves (optional)

1 Preheat indoor electric grill. For raita, in a small bowl combine yogurt, cucumber, onion, the snipped mint, and sugar. Season to taste with salt and pepper; set aside.

2 Trim fat from steak. Sprinkle steak with lemon-pepper seasoning. Place steak on the grill rack. If using a covered grill, close lid. Grill until steak is desired doneness. (For a covered grill, allow 5 to 7 minutes for medium rare or 7 to 9 minutes for medium. For an uncovered grill, allow 12 to 15 minutes for medium rare or 15 to 18 minutes for medium, turning once halfway through grilling.)

3 Thinly slice steak across the grain. If desired, arrange steak slices on mint leaves. Top with raita.

Nutrition Facts per serving: 237 cal., 10 g total fat (4 g sat. fat), 77 mg chol., 235 mg sodium, 5 g carbo., 0 g fiber, 29 g pro.
Daily Values: 1% vit. A, 3% vit. C, 10% calcium, 21% iron

Lettuce-Wrapped Vietnamese Beef

Vietnamese cuisine is becoming increasingly popular, and this fresh, flavorful dish makes it easy to see why. To eat, wrap the lettuce leaves around the beef slices and use your hands.

Prep: 15 minutes **Marinate:** 2 hours **Grill:** 5 minutes (covered) or 12 minutes (uncovered) **Serves:** 4

1   pound boneless beef top sirloin steak, cut 1 inch thick

Marinade

¼   cup chopped green onions
2   stalks lemongrass, chopped
2   tablespoons sugar
2   tablespoons lime juice
2   tablespoons fish sauce
3   cloves garlic, minced

1   recipe Rice Vinegar Sauce
8   large lettuce leaves
    Assorted toppings (such as shredded carrot, fresh cilantro leaves, shredded fresh mint, and/or chopped peanuts)

1 Trim fat from steak. Place steak in a plastic bag set in a shallow dish. For marinade, in a small bowl combine green onions, lemongrass, sugar, lime juice, fish sauce, and garlic. Pour over steak; seal bag. Marinate in the refrigerator for 2 to 24 hours, turning bag occasionally.

2 Preheat indoor electric grill. Drain steak, discarding marinade. Place steak on the grill rack. If using a covered grill, close lid. Grill until steak is desired doneness. (For a covered grill, allow 5 to 7 minutes for medium rare or 7 to 9 minutes for medium. For an uncovered grill, allow 12 to 15 minutes for medium rare or 15 to 18 minutes for medium, turning once halfway through grilling.)

3 Meanwhile, prepare Rice Vinegar Sauce. To serve, overlap 2 lettuce leaves on each of 4 dinner plates. Thinly slice steak across the grain. Arrange steak slices on lettuce leaves. Add the desired toppings; drizzle with sauce. Roll the lettuce leaves around steak slices.

Rice Vinegar Sauce: Combine ¼ cup sugar; ¼ cup rice vinegar; 2 tablespoons lime juice; 2 tablespoons fish sauce; 2 cloves garlic, minced; and dash ground red pepper. Makes about ½ cup.

Nutrition Facts per serving: 348 cal., 13 g total fat (5 g sat. fat), 76 mg chol., 671 mg sodium, 30 g carbo., 1 g fiber, 29 g pro.
Daily Values: 43% vit. A, 19% vit. C, 3% calcium, 28% iron

Mediterranean Steak & Vegetables

The marinade for these kabobs infuses sirloin with the herbs and the zest of the Mediterranean. Don't forget the cucumber-yogurt sauce known as tzatziki; it's simple yet delicious.

Prep: 30 minutes **Marinate:** 2 hours **Grill:** 3 minutes (covered) or 5 minutes (uncovered) **Serves:** 2

8 ounces boneless beef top sirloin steak, cut 1 inch thick

½ cup red and/or green sweet pepper cut into 1-inch pieces

1 small red onion, cut into wedges

Marinade

½ cup bottled Italian salad dressing

1 teaspoon dried oregano, crushed

¼ teaspoon black pepper

Sauce

⅓ cup chopped cucumber

⅓ cup plain low-fat yogurt

1 small clove garlic, minced
Dash salt

2 large pita bread rounds, halved crosswise and warmed*

1 Trim fat from steak. Cut steak into ¼-inch strips. Place the steak strips, sweet pepper pieces, and onion wedges in a plastic bag set in a shallow dish. For marinade, in a small bowl combine salad dressing, oregano, and black pepper. Pour over steak and vegetables; seal bag. Marinate in the refrigerator for 2 to 8 hours, turning bag occasionally.

2 Meanwhile, for sauce, stir together the cucumber, yogurt, garlic, and salt. Cover and refrigerate until ready to serve.

3 Preheat indoor electric grill. Drain steak and vegetables, discarding marinade. On eight 6-inch skewers, alternately thread the steak strips, sweet pepper pieces, and onion wedges, leaving ¼ inch between pieces.

4 Place kabobs on the grill rack. If using a covered grill, close lid. Grill until steak is slightly pink in center. (For a covered grill, allow 3 to 4 minutes. For an uncovered grill, allow 5 to 7 minutes, turning once halfway through grilling.) To serve, remove steak and vegetables from skewers. Fill warm pita halves with steak and vegetables. Top with sauce.

Nutrition Facts per serving: 540 cal., 24 g total fat (5 g sat. fat), 56 mg chol., 791 mg sodium, 46 g carbo., 3 g fiber, 33 g pro.
Daily Values: 23% vit. A, 124% vit. C, 17% calcium, 26% iron

*Note: To warm pita bread, wrap in microwave-safe paper towels and microwave on 100% power (high) for 30 to 45 seconds.

Italian Steak Sandwiches `SMALL GRILL`

Flavors of Italian cuisine dominate this sandwich. The intense garlic-olive oil sauce here elevates the steak sandwich from ordinary to outstanding.

Prep: 20 minutes **Grill:** 5 minutes (covered) or 12 minutes (uncovered) **Serves:** 2

Sauce

- ½ cup loosely packed fresh Italian flat-leaf parsley
- 1 tablespoon olive oil
- 2 teaspoons lemon juice
- 1½ teaspoons capers, drained
- 1 teaspoon water
- 1 clove garlic, minced
  Dash salt
  Dash bottled hot pepper sauce

- 8 ounces boneless beef sirloin steak, cut 1 inch thick
- 2 lettuce leaves
- ½ of a small onion, thinly sliced and separated into rings
- 2 1-inch slices sourdough or French bread, toasted

1 Preheat indoor electric grill. For sauce, in a blender container or food processor bowl combine parsley, olive oil, lemon juice, capers, water, garlic, salt, and hot pepper sauce. Cover and blend or process until nearly smooth, stopping and scraping sides as necessary. Set aside.

2 Trim fat from steak. Place steak on the grill rack. If using a covered grill, close lid. Grill until steak is desired doneness. (For a covered grill, allow 5 to 7 minutes for medium rare or 7 to 9 minutes for medium. For an uncovered grill, allow 12 to 15 minutes for medium rare or 15 to 18 minutes for medium, turning once halfway through grilling.)

3 Thinly slice steak across the grain. Arrange lettuce leaves and onion rings on bread slices; top with steak slices and sauce.

Nutrition Facts per serving: 284 cal., 12 g total fat (2 g sat. fat), 53 mg chol., 372 mg sodium, 16 g carbo., 2 g fiber, 27 g pro.
Daily Values: 8% vit. A, 41% vit. C, 7% calcium, 23% iron

Beef & Fruit Salad ♥

For an exotic presentation, serve the fruit part of this recipe in the shell of a kiwano (kee-WAH-noh) fruit. Kiwano has a jellylike pulp with a tart, yet sweet banana-cucumber flavor.

Prep: 20 minutes **Marinate:** 30 minutes **Grill:** 5 minutes (covered) or 12 minutes (uncovered) **Serves:** 4

12 ounces boneless beef
      sirloin steak, cut 1 inch
      thick

Marinade

⅓ cup reduced-sodium
      teriyaki sauce or soy
      sauce
¼ cup lemon juice
¼ cup water
 2 teaspoons toasted
      sesame oil
⅛ teaspoon bottled hot
      pepper sauce

 3 cups shredded napa
      cabbage
 1 cup torn or shredded
      sorrel or spinach
 2 cups fresh fruit (such as
      cut-up plums, nectarines,
      or kiwi fruit; halved
      seedless grapes or
      strawberries; raspberries;
      and/or blueberries)
 2 kiwanos (optional)

1 Trim fat from steak. Place steak in a plastic bag set in a
  shallow dish. For marinade, in a small bowl combine teriyaki
sauce, lemon juice, water, oil, and hot pepper sauce. Reserve
⅓ cup for dressing. Pour remaining marinade over steak; seal bag.
Marinate at room temperature for 30 minutes, turning bag
occasionally. (Or, marinate in the refrigerator up to 8 hours.)

2 Preheat indoor electric grill. Drain steak, discarding marinade.
  Place steak on the grill rack. If using a covered grill, close
lid. Grill until steak is desired doneness. (For a covered grill,
allow 5 to 7 minutes for medium rare or 7 to 9 minutes
for medium. For an uncovered grill, allow 12 to 15 minutes for
medium rare or 15 to 18 minutes for medium, turning once
halfway through grilling.)

3 To serve, divide cabbage and sorrel among 4 dinner plates.
  Thinly slice steak diagonally across the grain. Arrange steak
and fruit on top of greens. (Or, if desired, serve fruit in kiwano
shells.) Drizzle with dressing (and, if desired, pulp of kiwano).

Nutrition Facts per serving: 248 cal., 10 g total fat (3 g sat. fat), 57 mg chol.,
307 mg sodium, 19 g carbo., 2 g fiber, 22 g pro.
Daily Values: 19% vit. A, 86% vit. C, 6% calcium, 19% iron

Note: To serve the fruit in kiwano shells, cut each kiwano in half
crosswise. Scoop out pulp. Fill the kiwano shells with fruit and set on
top of greens. If desired, spoon the kiwano pulp over salads.

Burgers

Spanish Meat Loaves

In this Chapter:

Currant-Glazed Pork Burgers

Currant jelly and cloves—favorites for flavoring the Christmas ham—go casual for everyday eating in these savory pork burgers. Choose leafy greens as a crisp accompaniment.

Prep: 15 minutes **Grill:** 5 minutes (covered) or 14 minutes (uncovered) **Serves:** 4

Sauce
- ¼ cup currant jelly
- 3 tablespoons catsup
- 1 tablespoon vinegar
- ⅛ teaspoon ground cinnamon
- Dash ground cloves

Burgers
- 1 slightly beaten egg
- 3 tablespoons fine dry bread crumbs
- 2 tablespoons chopped onion
- 2 tablespoons milk
- ¼ teaspoon salt
- ¼ teaspoon dried thyme, crushed
- ⅛ teaspoon pepper
- 1 pound lean ground pork

- 4 lettuce leaves
- 4 whole wheat hamburger buns, split and toasted

1 For sauce, in a small saucepan combine currant jelly, catsup, vinegar, cinnamon, and cloves. Cook and stir just until boiling. Remove from heat and keep warm.

2 Preheat indoor electric grill. For burgers, in a medium bowl combine egg, bread crumbs, onion, milk, salt, thyme, and pepper. Add ground pork; mix lightly but thoroughly. Shape into four ¾-inch-thick patties.

3 Place patties on the grill rack. If using a covered grill, close lid. Grill patties until meat is no longer pink. (For a covered grill, allow 5 to 7 minutes. For an uncovered grill, allow 14 to 18 minutes, turning once halfway through grilling.)

4 Arrange lettuce on bottom halves of buns. Top with burgers, sauce, and top halves of buns.

Nutrition Facts per serving: 347 cal., 11 g total fat (4 g sat. fat), 107 mg chol., 612 mg sodium, 43 g carbo., 3 g fiber, 21 g pro.
Daily Values: 5% vit. A, 6% vit. C, 6% calcium, 18% iron

Pepper-Bacon Burgers

A word to the wise: When handling chile peppers, wear plastic gloves to keep the heat in the meat and off your hands.

Prep: 15 minutes **Grill:** 5 minutes (covered) or 14 minutes (uncovered) **Serves:** 4

1 small onion, thinly sliced and separated into rings
1 fresh Anaheim or mild green chile pepper, seeded and cut into rings
2 tablespoons margarine

Burgers

1 slightly beaten egg
¼ cup fine dry bread crumbs
6 slices crisp-cooked bacon, crumbled
4 to 6 fresh serrano peppers, seeded and finely chopped
2 tablespoons milk
1 pound lean ground beef

4 kaiser rolls or hamburger buns, split and toasted
4 lettuce leaves

1 In a small saucepan cook onion and Anaheim pepper in hot margarine about 5 minutes or until onion is tender.

2 Meanwhile, preheat indoor electric grill. For burgers, in a medium bowl combine egg, bread crumbs, bacon, serrano peppers, and milk. Add ground beef; mix lightly but thoroughly. Shape into four ¾-inch-thick patties.

3 Place patties on the grill rack. If using a covered grill, close lid. Grill patties until meat is no longer pink. (For a covered grill, allow 5 to 7 minutes. For an uncovered grill, allow 14 to 18 minutes, turning once halfway through grilling.) Serve burgers on rolls with onion mixture and lettuce leaves.

Nutrition Facts per serving: 550 cal., 29 g total fat (9 g sat. fat), 132 mg chol., 733 mg sodium, 38 g carbo., 1 g fiber, 32 g pro.
Daily Values: 11% vit. A, 34% vit. C, 8% calcium, 29% iron

toasting bread or buns

When I grill burgers, chicken breasts, or other meats for sandwiches, I use my indoor grill to toast the bread slices, hamburger buns, or kaiser rolls that I'm planning to use. It makes the sandwiches taste so much better!

Just before the meat is done (or as soon as you've removed the grilled meat if there's not enough room on your grill rack for both the meat and the bread), place the bread or split buns, cut sides down, on the rack of the hot grill. If you're using a covered grill, close lid. Grill until lightly toasted. (For a covered grill, allow 1 to 2 minutes. For an uncovered grill, allow 2 to 4 minutes, turning bread slices once halfway through grilling.)

Patty Bubout
Test Kitchen Home Economist

Sun-Dried Tomato Burgers

Burgers on the grill take on a whole new life when they're infused with fresh lemon, studded with dried tomatoes, and slathered with a zippy basil mayonnaise dressing.

Prep: 15 minutes **Grill:** 5 minutes (covered) or 14 minutes (uncovered) **Serves:** 4

Burgers

- 1 pound lean ground beef
- 1 tablespoon finely chopped, oil-packed dried tomatoes
- 1 teaspoon finely shredded lemon peel or lime peel
- ½ teaspoon salt
- ¼ teaspoon black pepper

- ¼ cup light mayonnaise dressing or salad dressing
- 2 tablespoons snipped fresh basil
- 1 fresh jalapeño pepper, seeded and finely chopped
- 4 onion hamburger buns, split and toasted
- 1 cup lightly packed arugula or spinach leaves

1 Preheat indoor electric grill. For burgers, in a medium bowl combine ground beef, dried tomatoes, lemon peel, salt, and black pepper; mix lightly but thoroughly. Shape into four ½-inch-thick patties.

2 Place patties on the grill rack. If using a covered grill, close lid. Grill patties until meat is no longer pink. (For a covered grill, allow 5 to 7 minutes. For an uncovered grill, allow 14 to 18 minutes, turning once halfway through grilling.)

3 Meanwhile, in a small bowl combine mayonnaise dressing, basil, and jalapeño pepper. Serve burgers on buns with mayonnaise mixture and arugula.

Nutrition Facts per serving: 450 cal., 20 g total fat (6 g sat. fat), 71 mg chol., 784 mg sodium, 40 g carbo., 2 g fiber, 26 g pro.
Daily Values: 1% vit. A, 13% vit. C, 6% calcium, 25% iron

Spanish Meat Loaves

Humble meat loaf goes haute cuisine, while retaining its universal appeal. These miniature loaves, flavored with green olives and glazed with jalapeño jelly, will charm their way into your repertoire.

Prep: 15 minutes **Grill:** 5 minutes (covered) or 14 minutes (uncovered) **Serves:** 4

Meat Loaves

- 1 slightly beaten egg
- ½ cup pimiento-stuffed green olives, sliced
- ⅓ cup quick-cooking rolled oats
- ¼ cup snipped fresh parsley
- ¼ cup tomato paste
- ¼ teaspoon pepper
- 1 pound lean ground beef

- ¼ cup jalapeño pepper jelly or apple jelly, melted

Relish

- 1 medium tomato, chopped
- ⅓ cup chunky salsa
- ¼ cup chopped, seeded cucumber
- 2 tablespoons sliced pimiento-stuffed green olives (optional)

- 8 thin slices bread, toasted (optional)
  Lettuce leaves

1 Preheat indoor electric grill. For meat loaves, in a medium bowl combine egg, the ½ cup olives, the rolled oats, parsley, tomato paste, and pepper. Add ground beef; mix lightly but thoroughly. Shape into four 4×3×¾-inch loaves.

2 Place meat loaves on the grill rack. If using a covered grill, close lid. Grill meat loaves until meat is no longer pink. (For a covered grill, allow 5 to 7 minutes, brushing with melted jelly after grilling. For an uncovered grill, allow 14 to 18 minutes, turning once halfway through and brushing with melted jelly the last 2 minutes of grilling.)

3 Meanwhile, for relish, in a small bowl combine the tomato, salsa, cucumber, and, if desired, the 2 tablespoons olives. Divide the bread slices (if desired) and lettuce among 4 dinner plates. Top with the meat loaves and relish.

Nutrition Facts per serving: 328 cal., 15 g total fat (5 g sat. fat), 125 mg chol., 437 mg sodium, 25 g carbo., 2 g fiber, 25 g pro.
Daily Values: 12% vit. A, 27% vit. C, 4% calcium, 20% iron

Indian Lamb Patties `SMALL GRILL`

Try these patties with one of the many Indian breads. Look for chapati (soft, unleavened, whole wheat bread); pappadam (thin lentil crackers); or naan (soft, yeasted flatbread baked in a clay oven).

Prep: 15 minutes **Grill:** 5 minutes (covered) or 14 minutes (uncovered) **Serves:** 2

Sauce
- ½ cup plain low-fat yogurt
- ⅓ cup chopped, seeded cucumber

Burgers
- ¼ cup finely chopped onion
- 1 fresh jalapeño pepper, seeded and chopped, or 2 tablespoons canned diced green chile peppers
- 1 tablespoon snipped fresh mint or 1 teaspoon dried mint, crushed
- ½ teaspoon ground cumin
- ½ teaspoon bottled minced garlic
- ¼ teaspoon salt
- 8 ounces lean ground lamb, pork, beef, or turkey

1 For sauce, in a small bowl stir together yogurt and cucumber. Cover and refrigerate until ready to serve.

2 Preheat indoor electric grill. For burgers, in a medium bowl combine onion, jalapeño pepper, mint, cumin, garlic, and salt. Add ground lamb; mix lightly but thoroughly. Shape into two ¾-inch-thick patties.

3 Place patties on the grill rack. If using a covered grill, close lid. Grill patties until meat is no longer pink. (For a covered grill, allow 5 to 7 minutes. For an uncovered grill, allow 14 to 18 minutes, turning once halfway through grilling.) Serve the burgers with sauce.

Nutrition Facts per serving: 332 cal., 22 g total fat (10 g sat. fat), 81 mg chol., 390 mg sodium, 9 g carbo., 1 g fiber, 23 g pro.
Daily Values: 3% vit. A, 15% vit. C, 15% calcium, 13% iron

lovin' that lamb

Years ago lamb had a strong flavor because sheep were bred to produce both wool and meat. Now, younger sheep, or lambs, are raised just for eating, and the meat is lean, tasty, and tender. There are, however, flavor and size differences between imported and domestic lamb. Domestic lamb often is milder than imported lamb because the animals are grain fed rather than grass fed. Also, lamb cuts from domestic animals are meatier and up to twice the size of the same cuts from imported animals—a result of differences in genetics and breeding techniques.

Zucchini Crab Cakes

You'll need to purchase 1 to 1¼ pounds of crab legs to get 8 ounces of cooked crabmeat. Be sure to clean crabmeat carefully, removing and discarding any small pieces of shell or cartilage.

Prep: 20 minutes **Grill:** 4 minutes (covered) or 6 minutes (uncovered) **Serves:** 4

1   recipe Tomato and Sour
     Cream Sauce
Crab Cakes
1   cup coarsely shredded
     zucchini
¼   cup thinly sliced green
     onions
2   teaspoons cooking oil
1   slightly beaten egg
½   cup seasoned fine dry
     bread crumbs
1   tablespoon Dijon-style
     mustard
½   teaspoon snipped fresh
     lemon thyme or thyme
⅛   to ¼ teaspoon ground red
     pepper (optional)
8   ounces cooked fresh
     crabmeat, chopped
     (1½ cups)

2   large red and/or yellow
     tomatoes, cut into
     ¼-inch slices
     Red and/or yellow cherry
     tomatoes (optional)
     Fresh chives (optional)

1 Prepare Tomato and Sour Cream Sauce. Cover and refrigerate up to 2 hours. For crab cakes, in a large skillet cook and stir zucchini and green onions in hot oil about 3 minutes or just until vegetables are tender and liquid is evaporated. Cool slightly.

2 Lightly grease the rack of an indoor electric grill or lightly coat with cooking spray. Preheat grill. In a large bowl combine the egg, bread crumbs, mustard, lemon thyme, and, if desired, red pepper. Add the zucchini mixture and crabmeat; mix well. Using about ¼ cup of the mixture for each crab cake, shape into eight ½-inch-thick patties.

3 Place patties on the grill rack. If using a covered grill, close lid. Grill until patties are golden brown. (For a covered grill, allow 4 to 6 minutes. For an uncovered grill, allow 6 to 8 minutes, turning once halfway through grilling.) Divide the crab cakes among 4 dinner plates. Serve with sliced tomatoes and sauce. If desired, garnish with cherry tomatoes and chives.

Tomato and Sour Cream Sauce: In a small bowl stir together ½ cup dairy sour cream, 3 tablespoons finely chopped yellow and/or red tomato, 1 to 2 tablespoons lemon juice or lime juice, and ⅛ teaspoon seasoned salt. Makes about ⅔ cup.

Nutrition Facts per serving: 237 cal., 12 g total fat (4 g sat. fat), 123 mg chol., 424 mg sodium, 16 g carbo., 2 g fiber, 17 g pro.
Daily Values: 17% vit. A, 39% vit. C, 10% calcium, 11% iron

Southwestern Chicken Burgers

Get along, little chicken burgers! These burgers obtain some of their Southwestern flair from nacho-flavored tortilla chips. Jack cheese, avocado slices, and salsa top them off.

Prep: 15 minutes **Grill:** 5 minutes (covered) or 14 minutes (uncovered) **Serves:** 4

Burgers

- 1 slightly beaten egg
- ¼ cup crushed nacho-flavored or plain tortilla chips
- 3 tablespoons finely chopped green sweet pepper
- ¾ teaspoon chili powder
- ¼ teaspoon salt
- ¼ teaspoon black pepper
- 1 pound uncooked ground chicken or turkey

- 4 ounces sliced Monterey Jack cheese with jalapeño peppers
- 1 avocado, seeded, peeled, and sliced
- 4 kaiser rolls or hamburger buns, split and toasted
  Lettuce leaves
  Salsa

1 Lightly grease the rack of an indoor electric grill or lightly coat with cooking spray. Preheat grill. For burgers, in a medium bowl combine egg, tortilla chips, sweet pepper, chili powder, salt, and black pepper. Add ground chicken; mix lightly but thoroughly. Shape into four ¾-inch-thick patties.

2 Place patties on the grill rack. If using a covered grill, close lid. Grill patties until chicken is no longer pink. (For a covered grill, allow 5 to 7 minutes. For an uncovered grill, allow 14 to 18 minutes, turning once halfway through grilling.)

3 Remove burgers from grill. Top burgers with cheese and avocado; let stand for 1 to 2 minutes or until cheese is melted. Serve burgers on rolls with lettuce and salsa.

Nutrition Facts per serving: 424 cal., 23 g total fat (9 g sat. fat), 133 mg chol., 674 mg sodium, 26 g carbo., 2 g fiber, 29 g pro.
Daily Values: 23% vit. A, 20% vit. C, 37% calcium, 20% iron

Cantonese Chicken Burgers

To make burger baskets, line a basket or bowl with a napkin and nestle the Oriental-style sandwiches in a bed of baked tortilla chips. For added color and flavor, garnish with orange wedges.

Prep: 15 minutes **Grill:** 5 minutes (covered) or 14 minutes (uncovered) **Serves:** 4

Burgers

- 1 slightly beaten egg
- 1 teaspoon toasted sesame oil
- 1 teaspoon soy sauce
- ⅓ cup fine dry bread crumbs
- ¼ cup chopped peanuts
- 2 tablespoons shredded carrot
- 1 green onion, thinly sliced
- ⅛ teaspoon garlic powder
- 1 pound uncooked ground chicken or turkey

- 4 sesame hamburger buns, split and toasted
- 8 spinach leaves, shredded
- ¼ cup plum sauce

1 Lightly grease the rack of an indoor electric grill or lightly coat with cooking spray. Preheat grill.

2 For burgers, in a medium bowl combine egg, sesame oil, and soy sauce. Stir in bread crumbs, peanuts, carrot, green onion, and garlic powder. Add ground chicken; mix lightly but thoroughly. Shape into four ¾-inch-thick patties.

3 Place patties on the grill rack. If using a covered grill, close lid. Grill patties until chicken is no longer pink. (For a covered grill, allow 5 to 7 minutes. For an uncovered grill, allow 14 to 18 minutes, turning once halfway through grilling.) Serve burgers on buns with shredded spinach and plum sauce.

Nutrition Facts per serving: 377 cal., 15 g total fat (3 g sat. fat), 108 mg chol., 429 mg sodium, 35 g carbo., 2 g fiber, 25 g pro.
Daily Values: 17% vit. A, 4% vit. C, 5% calcium, 17% iron

buying ground chicken

You can now find uncooked ground chicken at most grocery meat counters, but it's hard to tell at a glance whether it's breast meat, dark meat, or both. To be sure you get what you want (the leanest choice is strictly breast meat without the skin), ask the butcher to grind it fresh for you. Or, do it yourself: You can grind up boneless chicken breasts in seconds using a food processor.

Tami Leonard
Test Kitchen Home Economist

Moroccan Turkey Burgers SMALL GRILL

Want to give your American turkey burger Moroccan flair? Just add raisins, almonds, aromatic coriander and cumin, and a fresh mint-infused sauce.

Prep: 20 minutes **Grill:** 5 minutes (covered) or 14 minutes (uncovered) **Serves:** 2

2 tablespoons regular or light dairy sour cream
½ teaspoon snipped fresh mint

Burgers

8 ounces uncooked ground turkey or chicken
2 tablespoons chopped raisins
1 tablespoon chopped slivered almonds
⅛ teaspoon salt
⅛ teaspoon ground coriander
⅛ teaspoon ground cumin
⅛ teaspoon coarsely ground pepper

2 sesame hamburger buns, split and toasted

1 In a small bowl combine the sour cream and mint. Cover and refrigerate until ready to serve. Lightly grease the rack of an indoor electric grill or lightly coat with cooking spray. Preheat grill.

2 For burgers, in a medium bowl combine ground turkey, raisins, almonds, salt, coriander, cumin, and pepper; mix lightly but thoroughly. Shape into two ¾-inch-thick patties.

3 Place patties on the grill rack. If using a covered grill, close lid. Grill patties until turkey is no longer pink. (For a covered grill, allow 5 to 7 minutes. For an uncovered grill, allow 14 to 18 minutes, turning once halfway through grilling.) Serve burgers on buns with sour cream mixture.

Nutrition Facts per serving: 336 cal., 16 g total fat (5 g sat. fat), 49 mg chol., 396 mg sodium, 28 g carbo., 1 g fiber, 20 g pro.
Daily Values: 3% vit. A, 1% vit. C, 6% calcium, 18% iron

Southwestern Black Bean Cakes ♥

These spicy bean cakes get their sensational flavor from a chipotle—a dried, smoked jalapeño pepper—that comes in adobo sauce, a Mexican melange of ground chile peppers, herbs, and vinegar.

Prep: 20 minutes **Grill:** 4 minutes (covered) or 8 minutes (uncovered) **Serves:** 4

Bean Cakes
- 2 slices whole wheat bread, torn
- 3 tablespoons fresh cilantro leaves
- 2 cloves garlic
- 1 15-ounce can black beans, rinsed and drained
- 1 7-ounce can chipotle peppers in adobo sauce
- 1 teaspoon ground cumin
- 1 slightly beaten egg

Guacamole
- ½ of a medium avocado, seeded and peeled
- 1 tablespoon lime juice

- 1 small plum tomato, chopped

1 Lightly grease the rack of an indoor electric grill or lightly coat with cooking spray. Preheat grill. For bean cakes, place torn bread in a food processor bowl.* Cover and process until bread resembles coarse crumbs (you should have about 1½ cups crumbs). Transfer crumbs to a large bowl and set aside.

2 Place cilantro and garlic in food processor bowl; cover and process until finely chopped. Add beans, 1 of the chipotle peppers, 1 to 2 teaspoons of the adobo sauce (reserve remaining peppers and sauce for another use), and cumin. Cover and process using several on/off pulses until a paste forms (mixture will not be smooth). Add to bread crumbs. Add egg; mix well. Using moistened hands, shape into four ½-inch-thick patties.

3 Place patties on the grill rack. If using a covered grill, close lid. Grill until patties are heated through. (For a covered grill, allow 4 to 5 minutes. For an uncovered grill, allow 8 to 10 minutes, turning once halfway through grilling.)

4 Meanwhile, for guacamole, in a small bowl mash avocado. Stir in lime juice; season to taste with salt and black pepper. Serve bean cakes with guacamole and tomato.

Nutrition Facts per serving: 178 cal., 7 g total fat (1 g sat. fat), 53 mg chol., 487 mg sodium, 25 g carbo., 9 g fiber, 11 g pro.
Daily Values: 9% vit. A, 12% vit. C, 7% calcium, 16% iron

*Note: If you do not have a food processor, use a blender to make the bread crumbs. Finely chop the cilantro, garlic, and chipotle pepper. Using a fork, mash the beans with chipotle pepper, adobo sauce, and cumin. In a large bowl combine crumbs, cilantro, garlic, bean mixture, and egg. Continue as directed above.

Chops

Southwest Chops with Corn Salsa

In this Chapter:

Margarita-Glazed Pork Chops SMALL GRILL ♥

You can use tequila or just fresh lime juice to make the glaze. Either way, the taste is reminiscent of Mexico's most beloved cocktail, the margarita.

Prep: 10 minutes **Grill:** 6 minutes (covered) or 12 minutes (uncovered) **Serves:** 2

Glaze

- 3 tablespoons orange marmalade
- 1 tablespoon tequila or lime juice
- 1 small fresh jalapeño pepper, seeded and finely chopped
- ½ teaspoon grated fresh ginger or ¼ teaspoon ground ginger

- 2 boneless pork loin chops, cut ¾ inch thick
  Snipped fresh cilantro
  Lime and orange wedges (optional)

1 For glaze, in a small bowl stir together the orange marmalade, tequila, jalapeño pepper, and ginger. Set aside. Preheat indoor electric grill. Trim fat from chops.

2 Place chops on the grill rack. If using a covered grill, close lid. Grill until chops are slightly pink in center and juices run clear. (For a covered grill, allow 6 to 8 minutes, brushing once with glaze the last 1 to 2 minutes of grilling. For an uncovered grill, allow 12 to 15 minutes, turning once halfway through and brushing frequently with glaze the last 5 minutes of grilling.)

3 To serve, sprinkle the chops with cilantro. If desired, garnish with lime and orange wedges.

Nutrition Facts per serving: 252 cal., 6 g total fat (2 g sat. fat), 66 mg chol., 65 mg sodium, 20 g carbo., 2 g fiber, 25 g pro.
Daily Values: 2% vit. A, 9% vit. C, 3% calcium, 6% iron

grilling pork the right way

There's nothing more delicious than tender, juicy pork right off the grill. To make sure your pork loin chops turn out that way, grill them only to medium doneness. Overcooking produces tough, tasteless meat that is robbed of its true juicy character. To tell when the chops are done, look for a blush of pink when you cut into the meat and plenty of savory clear juices.

Colleen Weeden
Test Kitchen Home Economist

Jamaican Chops with Melon Salsa ♥

The jerk cooks of Jamaica may use dry rubs or wet marinades, but the central ingredient in all jerk seasoning is allspice, which grows in abundance on the sunny island.

Prep: 15 minutes **Grill:** 6 minutes (covered) or 12 minutes (uncovered) **Serves:** 4

Salsa

1 cup chopped honeydew melon
1 cup chopped cantaloupe
1 tablespoon snipped fresh mint
1 tablespoon honey

4 boneless pork top loin chops, cut ¾ inch thick
4 teaspoons Jamaican jerk seasoning
Fresh mint sprigs and/or star anise (optional)

1 For salsa, in a medium bowl combine honeydew melon, cantaloupe, the snipped mint, and the honey. Cover and refrigerate until ready to serve.

2 Preheat indoor electric grill. Trim fat from chops. Sprinkle jerk seasoning evenly over chops; rub in with your fingers.

3 Place chops on the grill rack. If using a covered grill, close lid. Grill until chops are slightly pink in center and juices run clear. (For a covered grill, allow 6 to 8 minutes. For an uncovered grill, allow 12 to 15 minutes, turning once halfway through grilling.) Serve the chops with salsa. If desired, garnish with mint sprigs and/or star anise.

Nutrition Facts per serving: 189 cal., 8 g total fat (3 g sat. fat), 51 mg chol., 231 mg sodium, 13 g carbo., 1 g fiber, 17 g pro.
Daily Values: 22% vit. A, 48% vit. C, 2% calcium, 10% iron

Apple-Sauced Chops

Most everyone is a fan of the famous duo—pork chops and applesauce. The "applesauce" here consists of apple, brown sugar, and cream, not only complementing the chops, but garnering center stage.

Prep: 20 minutes **Grill:** 6 minutes (covered) or 12 minutes (uncovered) **Serves:** 4

1 teaspoon ground cinnamon
½ teaspoon dried thyme, crushed
¼ teaspoon onion salt
¼ teaspoon dry mustard
4 boneless pork loin chops, cut ¾ inch thick

Sauce

2 tablespoons margarine or butter
1 medium onion, cut into thin wedges
1 large cooking apple (such as Rome Beauty), cored and thinly sliced
1 tablespoon brown sugar
½ cup whipping cream

1 In a small bowl stir together the cinnamon, thyme, onion salt, and dry mustard. Trim fat from chops. Sprinkle cinnamon mixture evenly over chops; rub in with your fingers. Set aside.

2 For sauce, in a medium skillet heat margarine over medium-low heat until melted; add onion. Cook, covered, for 13 to 15 minutes or until onion is tender. Uncover; add apple slices and brown sugar. Cook and stir over medium-high heat about 5 minutes or until onion is golden and apple is tender. Carefully stir in whipping cream. Bring just to boiling; reduce heat. Boil gently, uncovered, for 2 to 3 minutes or until slightly thickened.

3 Meanwhile, preheat indoor electric grill. Place chops on the grill rack. If using a covered grill, close lid. Grill until chops are slightly pink in center and juices run clear. (For a covered grill, allow 6 to 8 minutes. For an uncovered grill, allow 12 to 15 minutes, turning once halfway through grilling.) Serve the chops with sauce.

Nutrition Facts per serving: 357 cal., 23 g total fat (10 g sat. fat), 107 mg chol., 233 mg sodium, 12 g carbo., 2 g fiber, 25 g pro.
Daily Values: 19% vit. A, 7% vit. C, 6% calcium, 7% iron

low-fat bonus

If you're interested in healthy cooking, the indoor electric grill is a great appliance. Fat drips away from the meat as it cooks on the grill, automatically cutting fat from your diet—quite a difference from panfried food swimming in fat. If you want to reduce your intake of calories, fat, and cholesterol even more, select lean cuts of meat and eat sensible portion sizes. To help you in your search for health-conscious recipes, look for the low-fat main dishes marked with a ♥ symbol—each has 10 grams or less of fat per serving.

Plum Good Pork Chops SMALL GRILL ♥

When robust ingredients such as plum preserves, soy, lemon juice, and spices hit the grill, they offer up a tantalizing fusion of flavors. Try this fruity sauce with grilled chicken or lamb, too.

Prep: 15 minutes **Grill:** 12 minutes (uncovered) **Serves:** 2

Sauce
2 tablespoons plum preserves or jam
1 green onion, thinly sliced
2 teaspoons soy sauce
1 teaspoon lemon juice
  Dash curry powder
  Dash ground cinnamon
  Dash ground red pepper

2 pork loin chops, cut ¾ inch thick*
1 small clove garlic, halved

1 For sauce, in a small saucepan combine preserves, green onion, soy sauce, lemon juice, curry powder, cinnamon, and red pepper. Cook and stir over medium heat just until bubbly. Remove from heat and set aside.

2 Preheat *uncovered* indoor electric grill. Trim fat from chops. Rub both sides of chops with cut sides of garlic. Place chops on the grill rack. Grill until chops are slightly pink in center and juices run clear. (Allow 12 to 15 minutes, turning once halfway through grilling.) Serve the chops with sauce.

Nutrition Facts per serving: 213 cal., 5 g total fat (2 g sat. fat), 62 mg chol., 362 mg sodium, 14 g carbo., 1 g fiber, 26 g pro.
Daily Values: 1% vit. A, 9% vit. C, 3% calcium, 5% iron

*Note: If you have a covered grill, substitute 2 boneless pork loin chops, cut ¾ inch thick, for the pork loin chops. Preheat grill. Place chops on the grill rack; close lid. Grill until slightly pink in center and juices run clear. (Allow 6 to 8 minutes.)

Southwest Chops with Corn Salsa ♥

In late summer, when corn is at its sweetest and tomatoes are at their juiciest, these meaty chops crowned with a colorful, chunky salsa are unsurpassed for the freshest tastes of the season's best.

Prep: 20 minutes   **Grill:** 6 minutes (covered) or 12 minutes (uncovered)   **Serves:** 4

Sauce
- ¼ cup white wine vinegar
- 3 tablespoons snipped fresh cilantro
- 1 teaspoon olive oil

Salsa
- 1 cup fresh or frozen whole kernel corn
- 3 plum tomatoes, chopped
- ½ cup thinly sliced green onions
- 1 small fresh jalapeño pepper, seeded and finely chopped

- 4 boneless pork loin chops, cut ¾ inch thick
- Cactus leaves (optional)
- Cilantro sprigs (optional)

1 For sauce, in a small bowl combine 3 tablespoons of the vinegar, 1 tablespoon of the snipped cilantro, and the oil. For salsa, in a covered small saucepan cook fresh corn in a small amount of boiling water for 2 to 3 minutes or until crisp-tender; drain. Or, thaw corn, if frozen. In a medium bowl combine corn, tomatoes, green onions, jalapeño pepper, the remaining vinegar, and the remaining snipped cilantro. Set aside.

2 Preheat indoor electric grill. Trim fat from chops. Place chops on the grill rack. If using a covered grill, close lid. Grill until chops are slightly pink in center and juices run clear. (For a covered grill, allow 6 to 8 minutes, brushing once with sauce the last 1 minute of grilling. For an uncovered grill, allow 12 to 15 minutes, turning once halfway through and brushing occasionally with sauce the last 5 minutes of grilling.) If desired, arrange chops on cactus leaves. Serve with salsa and, if desired, garnish with cilantro sprigs.

Nutrition Facts per serving: 201 cal., 9 g total fat (3 g sat. fat), 51 mg chol., 51 mg sodium, 14 g carbo., 2 g fiber, 18 g pro.
Daily Values: 7% vit. A, 35% vit. C, 0% calcium, 8% iron

Teriyaki Pork Salad

In Japanese "teri" means glazed and "yaki" means baked or broiled. The sugar in the marinade caramelizes during grilling, giving the pork a beautiful shine.

Prep: 15 minutes **Marinate:** 20 minutes **Grill:** 6 minutes (covered) or 12 minutes (uncovered) **Serves:** 4

4 boneless pork top loin chops, cut ¾ inch thick

Marinade

⅓ cup rice vinegar
⅓ cup orange juice
2 tablespoons reduced-sodium teriyaki sauce
1 tablespoon peanut oil or salad oil
1 teaspoon sesame seed, toasted
1 teaspoon bottled minced garlic

6 cups torn mixed salad greens
¾ cup sliced red radishes
¼ cup thinly sliced green onions

1 Trim fat from chops. Place chops in a plastic bag set in a shallow dish. For marinade, in a medium bowl whisk together vinegar, orange juice, teriyaki sauce, oil, sesame seed, and garlic. Reserve half for dressing. Pour the remaining marinade over chops; seal bag. Marinate in the refrigerator at least 20 minutes or up to 8 hours, turning bag occasionally.

2 Preheat indoor electric grill. Drain chops, discarding marinade. Place chops on the grill rack. If using a covered grill, close lid. Grill until chops are slightly pink in center and juices run clear. (For a covered grill, allow 6 to 8 minutes. For an uncovered grill, allow 12 to 15 minutes, turning once halfway through grilling.)

3 Divide the salad greens, radishes, and green onions among 4 dinner plates. Thinly slice pork diagonally and arrange on top of greens. Drizzle with dressing.

Nutrition Facts per serving: 199 cal., 11 g total fat (3 g sat. fat), 51 mg chol., 172 mg sodium, 7 g carbo., 1 g fiber, 18 g pro.
Daily Values: 4% vit. A, 28% vit. C, 2% calcium, 8% iron

make mine marinated

Marinating meat, which is really nothing more than soaking it in a seasoned liquid, not only adds flavor, but makes the meat more tender. Usually marinades are made with an acidic liquid (providing the tenderizing effect) such as wine, vinegar, or citrus juice, plus herbs and seasonings—and sometimes a little oil. The longer the meat spends luxuriating in the liquid, the more great taste it will have.

Jan Miller

Test Kitchen Home Economist

Lamb Chops with Fruit Sauce `SMALL GRILL`

Tender, succulent lamb tastes even better when accompanied with fruit and mint. We dressed up these chops with a sauce made from orange juice, dried fruit bits, and fresh sprigs of mint.

Prep: 10 minutes   **Grill:** 6 minutes (covered) or 12 minutes (uncovered)   **Serves:** 2

Sauce

1	teaspoon sugar
1	teaspoon snipped fresh mint or ¼ teaspoon dried mint, crushed
½	teaspoon cornstarch
	Dash salt
½	cup orange juice
¼	cup mixed dried fruit bits

4	lamb loin chops, cut 1 inch thick (about 1 pound total)
	Fresh mint sprigs (optional)

1 For sauce, in a small saucepan combine sugar, dried mint (if using), cornstarch, and salt. Stir in orange juice. Cook and stir over medium heat until thickened and bubbly. If using, stir in snipped fresh mint. Cook and stir for 2 minutes more. Remove from heat. Reserve 2 tablespoons for basting. Stir dried fruit into the remaining sauce; cover and keep warm.

2 Preheat indoor electric grill. Trim fat from chops. Place chops on the grill rack. If using a covered grill, close lid.* Grill until chops are desired doneness. (For a covered grill, allow 6 to 8 minutes for medium, brushing once with the reserved sauce the last 1 to 2 minutes of grilling. For an uncovered grill, allow 12 to 15 minutes for medium, turning and brushing once with the reserved sauce halfway through grilling.)

3 Serve lamb chops with the fruit sauce. If desired, garnish with fresh mint sprigs.

Nutrition Facts per serving: 344 cal., 12 g total fat (4 g sat. fat), 114 mg chol., 180 mg sodium, 21 g carbo., 0 g fiber, 37 g pro.
Daily Values: 4% vit. A, 37% vit. C, 2% calcium, 20% iron

*Note: When cooking in a covered grill, it is important to use chops of the same thickness so the lid will sit evenly and close completely. If the lid does not fit tightly over the chops, you'll need to turn the chops once halfway through grilling.

Lamb with Sweet Potato Chutney

Petite lamb chops make simple yet pretty company fare—especially when they're crowned with a richly colored, flavor-packed homemade chutney.

Prep: 20 minutes **Grill:** 6 minutes (covered) or 12 minutes (uncovered) **Serves:** 4

8 lamb rib or loin chops, cut 1 inch thick
⅓ cup finely chopped shallots
¼ teaspoon crushed red pepper

Chutney
¼ cup packed brown sugar
¼ cup vinegar
2 tablespoons dried cranberries or currants
½ teaspoon grated fresh ginger
1 medium sweet potato, peeled and cubed

1 Preheat indoor electric grill. Trim fat from chops. In a small bowl combine shallots and red pepper. Reserve 2 tablespoons for chutney. Sprinkle the remaining shallot mixture evenly over chops; rub in with your fingers.

2 Place chops on the grill rack. If using a covered grill, close lid.* Grill until chops are desired doneness. (For a covered grill, allow 6 to 8 minutes for medium. For an uncovered grill, allow 12 to 15 minutes for medium, turning once halfway through grilling.)

3 Meanwhile, for chutney, in a medium saucepan combine the reserved shallot mixture, the brown sugar, vinegar, dried cranberries, and ginger. Stir in sweet potato. Bring to boiling; reduce heat. Simmer, covered, for 10 minutes, stirring occasionally. Serve the chops with chutney.

Nutrition Facts per serving: 317 cal., 11 g total fat (4 g sat. fat), 97 mg chol., 83 mg sodium, 24 g carbo., 1 g fiber, 30 g pro.
Daily Values: 81% vit. A, 13% vit. C, 3% calcium, 22% iron

***Note:** When cooking in a covered grill, it is important to use chops of the same thickness so the lid will sit evenly and close completely. If the lid does not fit tightly over the chops, you'll need to turn the chops once halfway through grilling.

Garlic Veal Chops

This lovely dish contains the essence of spring (asparagus and thyme) and the essence of taste (sherry and garlic) in one. It's simple enough for weeknight dining, but special enough to serve guests.

Prep: 15 minutes **Marinate:** 30 minutes **Grill:** 6 minutes (covered) or 10 minutes (uncovered) **Serves:** 4

1 pound asparagus spears
2 tablespoons dry sherry
2 tablespoons olive oil
1 clove garlic, minced
4 boneless veal top loin chops, cut ¾ inch thick
3 or 4 cloves garlic, cut into thin slivers
1 tablespoon snipped fresh thyme or 1 teaspoon dried thyme, crushed
⅛ teaspoon salt
⅛ teaspoon pepper

1 Snap off and discard woody stems from asparagus spears. In a medium skillet bring a small amount of water to boiling; add asparagus. Simmer, covered, for 3 minutes; drain. Place asparagus in a plastic bag. Add sherry, 1 tablespoon of the olive oil, and the minced garlic; seal bag. Marinate at room temperature for 30 minutes, turning bag occasionally.

2 Preheat indoor electric grill. Trim fat from chops. With the tip of a paring knife, make small slits in chops; insert garlic slivers in slits. Combine the remaining olive oil, the thyme, salt, and pepper; brush over chops.

3 Place chops on the grill rack. If using a covered grill, close lid. Grill until chops are desired doneness. (For a covered grill, allow 4 to 5 minutes for medium. For an uncovered grill, allow 7 to 9 minutes for medium, turning once halfway through grilling.) Remove from grill; cover and keep warm.

4 Add asparagus to the grill rack. If using a covered grill, close lid. Grill until asparagus is crisp-tender and light brown. (For a covered grill, allow 2 to 4 minutes. For an uncovered grill, allow 3 to 5 minutes, turning occasionally to cook evenly.) Serve the chops with asparagus.

Nutrition Facts per serving: 237 cal., 11 g total fat (3 g sat. fat), 92 mg chol., 131 mg sodium, 5 g carbo., 2 g fiber, 27 g pro.
Daily Values: 6% vit. A, 37% vit. C, 2% calcium, 9% iron

Jambalaya Smoked Pork Chops ♥

Serving grilled pork chops with a New Orleans-style jambalaya sauce is the perfect way to bring on some bayou-style fun.

Prep: 15 minutes **Grill:** 6 minutes (covered) or 12 minutes (uncovered) **Serves:** 4

4 smoked boneless pork loin chops, cut ¾ inch thick
¼ teaspoon black pepper
½ of a medium onion, cut into 1-inch pieces
½ of a medium green sweet pepper, cut into 1-inch pieces

Sauce
1 cup water
1 tablespoon cornstarch
½ teaspoon instant chicken bouillon granules
1 14½-ounce can Cajun-style stewed tomatoes

1 tablespoon snipped fresh parsley
2 cups hot cooked brown rice

1 Trim fat from chops. Sprinkle chops with black pepper; set aside. On two 6-inch skewers, thread onion and sweet pepper, leaving ¼ inch between pieces.

2 Lightly grease the rack of an indoor electric grill or lightly coat with cooking spray. Preheat grill. Place kabobs on the grill rack. If using a covered grill, close lid. Grill for 2 minutes on a covered grill or for 4 minutes on an uncovered grill, turning occasionally to cook evenly.

3 Add chops to the grill rack. If using a covered grill, close lid. Grill until chops are heated through and vegetables are tender. (For a covered grill, allow 4 to 6 minutes. For an uncovered grill, allow 8 to 11 minutes, turning chops once halfway through grilling and turning kabobs occasionally.) Remove from grill. Cover chops and keep warm. Coarsely chop vegetables; set aside.

4 For sauce, in a large saucepan combine water, cornstarch, and bouillon granules. Stir in undrained tomatoes (snip any large pieces). Cook and stir over medium heat until thickened and bubbly. Cook and stir for 2 minutes more. Stir in the chopped vegetables; heat through.

5 To serve, spoon the sauce over chops and sprinkle with parsley. Serve with brown rice.

Nutrition Facts per serving: 210 cal., 6 g total fat (2 g sat. fat), 51 mg chol., 1,202 mg sodium, 19 g carbo., 0 g fiber, 20 g pro.
Daily Values: 0% vit. A, 34% vit. C, 1% calcium, 11% iron

Chicken & Turkey

Chicken Mole Sandwich

In this Chapter:

Chicken with Mango Chutney ♥

There are a variety of chutneys available on the market, but homemade is best. Who would have guessed something so exotic could be so easy to make?

Prep: 20 minutes **Grill:** 4 minutes (covered) or 12 minutes (uncovered) **Serves:** 4

1	ripe mango, seeded, peeled, and sliced
¼	cup dried currants or raisins
¼	cup thinly sliced green onions
2 to 3	tablespoons cider vinegar
2	tablespoons brown sugar
½	teaspoon mustard seed, crushed
⅛	teaspoon salt
1	teaspoon five-spice powder
1	pound skinless, boneless chicken thighs

1 In a medium saucepan combine half of the mango slices, the currants, green onions, vinegar, brown sugar, mustard seed, and salt. Bring to boiling; reduce heat. Simmer, covered, for 5 minutes. Remove from heat. Lightly grease the rack of an indoor electric grill or lightly coat with cooking spray. Preheat grill.

2 Meanwhile, chop remaining mango slices; set aside. Sprinkle five-spice powder evenly over chicken; rub in with your fingers. Place chicken on the grill rack. If using a covered grill, close lid. Grill until chicken is tender and no longer pink. (For a covered grill, allow 4 to 6 minutes. For an uncovered grill, allow 12 to 15 minutes, turning once halfway through grilling.) Stir chopped mango into cooked mango mixture. Serve with chicken.

Nutrition Facts per serving: 205 cal., 6 g total fat (2 g sat. fat), 54 mg chol., 125 mg sodium, 22 g carbo., 2 g fiber, 17 g pro.
Daily Values: 22% vit. A, 26% vit. C, 3% calcium, 10% iron

slick uses for your indoor grill

Once I started using my indoor grill, I was amazed at how versatile it is. Besides using it to grill main dishes, I rely on it to speed up other cooking chores. Here are a few:

● When a recipe calls for cooked chicken, use the indoor electric grill to turn out tender, moist chicken in just minutes.

● Use the grill to make easy grilled cheese sandwiches. You can also warm up other sandwiches by toasting them lightly on the grill.

● For an easy sandwich topping, grill onion slices and sweet pepper strips on the grill and sprinkle them with balsamic vinegar.

● Cook bacon on the grill. Add it to sandwiches or crumble over salads or cooked veggies.

Jill Moberly

Test Kitchen Home Economist

Chicken with Burgundy Sauce SMALL GRILL ♥

Grilled chicken breasts become wonderfully fruity with an orange and burgundy sauce. Add herbed or regular linguine and finish with a scoop of sorbet for an elegant yet simple meal.

Prep: 10 minutes **Grill:** 4 minutes (covered) or 12 minutes (uncovered) **Serves:** 2

Sauce
- 2 tablespoons orange marmalade
- ¼ teaspoon cornstarch
- ⅛ teaspoon salt
- 2 tablespoons burgundy

- 2 medium skinless, boneless chicken breast halves (about 8 ounces total)
- Hot cooked pasta (optional)
- Fresh thyme sprigs (optional)
- Orange slices (optional)

1 Lightly grease the rack of an indoor electric grill or lightly coat with cooking spray. Preheat grill. For sauce, in a small saucepan combine orange marmalade, cornstarch, and salt. Stir in burgundy. Cook and stir until mixture is thickened and bubbly. Cook and stir for 1 minute more. Set aside.

2 Place chicken on the grill rack. If using a covered grill, close lid. Grill until chicken is tender and no longer pink. (For a covered grill, allow 4 to 6 minutes. For an uncovered grill, allow 12 to 15 minutes, turning once halfway through grilling.)

3 To serve, spoon the sauce over chicken. If desired, serve with pasta and garnish with thyme sprigs and orange slices.

Nutrition Facts per serving: 184 cal., 3 g total fat (1 g sat. fat), 59 mg chol., 199 mg sodium, 15 g carbo., 1 g fiber, 22 g pro.
Daily Values: 0% vit. A, 2% vit. C, 1% calcium, 6% iron

Raspberry Chicken with Plantains ♥

The plantain is the starchier, less-sweet cousin of the beloved banana. Unlike bananas, though, plantains must be cooked before eaten. Here they're sautéed with a little brown sugar and vinegar.

Prep: 25 minutes **Grill:** 4 minutes (covered) or 12 minutes (uncovered) **Serves:** 4

Sauce

- 1 cup fresh raspberries (½ pint) or one 10-ounce package frozen unsweetened raspberries
- 2 tablespoons granulated sugar
- 1 teaspoon margarine or butter
- 2 ripe plantains or firm bananas, sliced
- 2 tablespoons brown sugar
- 2 tablespoons white wine vinegar
- 2 green onions, thinly sliced
- 1 small fresh jalapeño pepper, seeded and finely chopped

- 4 medium skinless, boneless chicken breast halves (about 1 pound total)
  Ti leaves (optional)

1 For sauce, in a small saucepan combine raspberries and granulated sugar. Heat over low heat about 3 minutes or until raspberries are softened. Press raspberries through a fine-mesh sieve; discard seeds.

2 In a large nonstick skillet heat margarine over medium heat. Add the plantains (if using); cook and stir about 2 minutes or until plantains are light brown and slightly softened. Stir in bananas (if using), brown sugar, and vinegar; heat through. Remove from heat. Stir in green onions and jalapeño pepper. Cover and keep warm.

3 Meanwhile, lightly grease the rack of an indoor electric grill or lightly coat with cooking spray. Preheat grill. Sprinkle chicken with salt and black pepper. Place chicken on the grill rack. If using a covered grill, close lid. Grill until chicken is tender and no longer pink. (For a covered grill, allow 4 to 6 minutes. For an uncovered grill, allow 12 to 15 minutes, turning once halfway through grilling.)

4 If desired, arrange chicken breasts on ti leaves. Serve the chicken with sauce and plantains.

Nutrition Facts per serving: 300 cal., 5 g total fat (1 g sat. fat), 59 mg chol., 103 mg sodium, 45 g carbo., 4 g fiber, 23 g pro.
Daily Values: 13% vit. A, 48% vit. C, 2% calcium, 11% iron

Apple-Glazed Chicken & Vegetables ♥

Pick your favorite apples for this innovative, sweet-and-savory dish. Either red or green apples work fine, but you want them to be tart. Good choices include Granny Smith, McIntosh, or Jonathan.

Prep: 20 minutes **Grill:** 4 minutes (covered) or 12 minutes (uncovered) **Serves:** 4

1 recipe Apple Glaze
2 medium apples, cored and coarsely chopped
1 medium leek, sliced, or ⅓ cup chopped onion
2 cloves garlic, minced
2 tablespoons apple cider or chicken broth
1 10-ounce bag prewashed spinach, stems removed (about 10 cups)
4 medium skinless, boneless chicken breast halves (about 1 pound total)

1 Prepare Apple Glaze; set aside. Lightly coat an unheated large saucepan or Dutch oven with cooking spray. Add apples, leek, and garlic. Cook over medium heat for 3 minutes, stirring occasionally. Add ¼ cup of the glaze and the apple cider; bring to boiling. Add the spinach; toss just until wilted. Remove from heat. Sprinkle with salt and pepper.

2 Meanwhile, lightly grease the rack of an indoor electric grill or lightly coat with cooking spray. Preheat grill. Place chicken on the grill rack. If using a covered grill, close lid. Grill until chicken is tender and no longer pink. (For a covered grill, allow 4 to 6 minutes, brushing once with glaze the last 1 minute of grilling. For an uncovered grill, allow 12 to 15 minutes, turning once halfway through and brushing frequently with glaze the last 5 minutes of grilling.)

3 To serve, slice chicken diagonally into strips. Divide spinach mixture among 4 dinner plates and top with chicken strips.

Apple Glaze: In a small saucepan combine ½ cup apple jelly; 2 tablespoons soy sauce; 1 tablespoon snipped fresh thyme or 1 teaspoon dried thyme, crushed; 1 teaspoon grated fresh ginger; and 1 teaspoon finely shredded lemon peel. Heat just until jelly is melted, stirring occasionally.

Nutrition Facts per serving: 300 cal., 2 g total fat (1 g sat. fat), 66 mg chol., 653 mg sodium, 40 g carbo., 9 g fiber, 30 g pro.
Daily Values: 39% vit. A, 42% vit. C, 9% calcium, 33% iron

Chicken Mole Sandwich

It's the mole (MOH-lay) that makes this sandwich a zinger. Would you believe a sauce of chocolate and Mexican chile peppers could taste this good?

Prep: 35 minutes **Grill:** 4 minutes (covered) or 12 minutes (uncovered) **Chill:** 30 minutes **Serves:** 4

Mole

- ¼ cup chopped onion
- 3 cloves garlic, minced
- 1 tablespoon cooking oil
- ½ cup water
- 3 dried chile peppers (New Mexico or pasilla), seeded and coarsely chopped
- 3 tablespoons chopped Mexican-style sweet chocolate or semisweet chocolate (1½ ounces)

- 4 medium skinless, boneless chicken breast halves (about 1 pound total)
- 1 small avocado, seeded, peeled, and mashed
- 2 tablespoons light mayonnaise dressing or salad dressing
- ⅛ teaspoon salt
- 4 large hard rolls, split and toasted
  Tomato slices
  Baby romaine lettuce or other lettuce leaves

1 For mole, in a large skillet cook onion and garlic in hot oil over medium-high heat until onion is tender. Add water and dried chile peppers. Reduce heat to medium; stir in chocolate. Cook and stir for 3 to 5 minutes or until thickened and bubbly. Cool slightly. Transfer mixture to a food processor bowl or blender container. Cover and process or blend until a smooth paste forms. Reserve 1 to 2 tablespoons for basting.

2 Lightly grease the rack of an indoor electric grill or lightly coat with cooking spray. Preheat grill. If desired, sprinkle chicken with salt. Using a sharp knife, cut a slit horizontally two-thirds of the way through each chicken piece. Spread chicken open; fill with remaining mole. Fold closed.

3 Place chicken on the grill rack. If using a covered grill, close lid. Grill until chicken is tender and no longer pink. (For a covered grill, allow 4 to 6 minutes, brushing once with the reserved mole the last 1 minute of grilling. For an uncovered grill, allow 12 to 15 minutes, turning once halfway through and brushing with the reserved mole the last 3 minutes of grilling.) Cover and refrigerate for 30 minutes.

4 Combine avocado, mayonnaise dressing, and ⅛ teaspoon salt. Cut chicken diagonally into ¼- to ½-inch slices. Spread avocado mixture on rolls; layer with tomato, chicken, and romaine.

Nutrition Facts per serving: 496 cal., 22 g total fat (5 g sat. fat), 59 mg chol., 542 mg sodium, 45 g carbo., 5 g fiber, 30 g pro.
Daily Values: 34% vit. A, 15% vit. C, 8% calcium, 29% iron

Grilled Vietnamese Chicken Breasts

This is no ho-hum chicken sandwich. Spicy-sweet peanut sauce and crisp broccoli slaw lend an Asian accent to this out-of-the-ordinary grilled chicken. If you like, top with a handful of chopped peanuts.

Prep: 15 minutes **Grill:** 4 minutes (covered) or 12 minutes (uncovered) **Serves:** 4

2 teaspoons toasted sesame oil

½ teaspoon crushed red pepper

4 medium skinless, boneless chicken breast halves (about 1 pound total)

Sauce

2 tablespoons sugar

2 tablespoons peanut butter

2 tablespoons soy sauce

2 tablespoons water

1 tablespoon cooking oil

1 clove garlic, minced

4 French-style rolls, split and toasted

½ cup packaged shredded broccoli (broccoli slaw mix)

1 Lightly grease the rack of an indoor electric grill or lightly coat with cooking spray. Preheat grill. Combine sesame oil and crushed red pepper; brush over both sides of chicken.

2 Place chicken on the grill rack. If using a covered grill, close lid. Grill until chicken is tender and no longer pink. (For a covered grill, allow 4 to 6 minutes. For an uncovered grill, allow 12 to 15 minutes, turning once halfway through grilling.)

3 Meanwhile, for sauce, in a small saucepan stir together sugar, peanut butter, soy sauce, water, cooking oil, and garlic. Heat until sugar is dissolved, stirring frequently. Serve chicken breasts on rolls with sauce and broccoli.

Nutrition Facts per serving: 360 cal., 14 g total fat (3 g sat. fat), 59 mg chol., 852 mg sodium, 29 g carbo., 1 g fiber, 28 g pro.
Daily Values: 3% vit. A, 14% vit. C, 4% calcium, 14% iron

sizzlin' sandwiches

Boneless chicken breasts are ideal for grilled sandwiches. Try these standbys:

● Toss chopped grilled chicken with a spoonful each of mayonnaise and pesto. Serve the mixture on hard rolls and top with tomato slices.

● Sprinkle boneless chicken breasts with Cajun seasoning; grill. Serve the breasts on toasted buns and top with sliced avocado.

● Marinate boneless chicken breasts in a little olive oil and balsamic vinegar; grill. Serve the chicken on toasted buns and top with roasted red sweet peppers and mayonnaise.

Oriental Chicken Kabobs `SMALL GRILL` ♥

To prevent a messy situation, it's best to thread the uncooked chicken on the skewers before you marinate the meat. At grilling time, simply drain the kabobs—no fuss!

Prep: 20 minutes **Marinate:** 4 hours **Grill:** 3 minutes (covered) or 8 minutes (uncovered) **Serves:** 2

8 ounces skinless, boneless chicken thighs

Marinade

2 tablespoons orange juice

1 tablespoon soy sauce

1 tablespoon dry sherry

½ teaspoon grated fresh ginger or ⅛ teaspoon ground ginger

Dash crushed red pepper

½ teaspoon sesame seed

Orange wedges (optional)

1 Cut chicken into thin strips. On 6-inch bamboo skewers, thread chicken, accordion-style. Place kabobs in a plastic bag set in a shallow dish. For marinade, in a small bowl combine orange juice, soy sauce, sherry, ginger, and crushed red pepper. Pour over kabobs; seal bag. Marinate in the refrigerator for 4 to 24 hours, turning bag occasionally.

2 Lightly grease the rack of an indoor electric grill or lightly coat with cooking spray. Preheat grill. Drain kabobs, discarding marinade. Place kabobs on the grill rack. If using a covered grill, close lid. Grill until chicken is tender and no longer pink. (For a covered grill, allow 3 to 5 minutes, sprinkling once with sesame seed halfway through grilling. For an uncovered grill, allow 8 to 10 minutes, turning and sprinkling once with sesame seed halfway through grilling.) If desired, garnish the kabobs with orange wedges.

Nutrition Facts per serving: 160 cal., 5 g total fat (1 g sat. fat), 91 mg chol., 308 mg sodium, 2 g carbo., 0 g fiber, 24 g pro.
Daily Values: 2% vit. A, 18% vit. C, 2% calcium, 7% iron

Chicken Fajitas with Guacamole

There's nothing flat about these tortillas filled with chili-crazed chicken strips. Serve a dish of guacamole on the side, and you're in Southwest heaven.

Prep: 25 minutes **Marinate:** 1 hour **Grill:** 4 minutes (covered) or 12 minutes (uncovered) **Serves:** 4

1 recipe Guacamole
3 medium skinless, boneless
   chicken breast halves
   (about 12 ounces total)

Marinade
¼ cup snipped fresh cilantro
   or parsley
¼ cup olive oil or cooking oil
1 teaspoon finely shredded
   lemon peel
2 tablespoons lemon juice
1 teaspoon chili powder
½ teaspoon ground cumin
½ teaspoon pepper

8 8-inch flour tortillas
2 cups shredded lettuce
1 cup shredded cheddar
   cheese (4 ounces)
1 large tomato, chopped
½ cup sliced pitted ripe
   olives

1 Prepare the Guacamole. Cover and refrigerate up to 4 hours. Place chicken in a shallow dish. For marinade, in a small bowl combine cilantro, oil, lemon peel, lemon juice, chili powder, cumin, and pepper. Pour over chicken; turn to coat. Cover and marinate in the refrigerator for 1 hour, turning chicken once. Stack tortillas and wrap in microwave-safe paper towels; set aside.

2 Lightly grease the rack of an indoor electric grill or lightly coat with cooking spray. Preheat grill. Drain chicken, discarding marinade. Place chicken on the grill rack. If using a covered grill, close lid. Grill until chicken is tender and no longer pink. (For a covered grill, allow 4 to 6 minutes. For an uncovered grill, allow 12 to 15 minutes, turning once halfway through grilling.) Microwave tortillas on 100% power (high) for 30 to 45 seconds or until warm.

3 To serve, slice chicken diagonally into bite-size strips. On each tortilla arrange chicken strips, lettuce, cheese, tomato, and olives. Fold in sides; roll up tortillas. Serve with guacamole.

Guacamole: Seed and peel 1 ripe avocado. In a small bowl coarsely mash avocado. Stir in 1 medium tomato, seeded, chopped, and drained; 2 tablespoons finely chopped onion; 1 tablespoon lemon juice; and ¼ teaspoon salt. Makes about ¾ cup.

Nutrition Facts per serving: 576 cal., 32 g total fat (10 g sat. fat), 74 mg chol., 745 mg sodium, 45 g carbo., 5 g fiber, 30 g pro.
Daily Values: 19% vit. A, 39% vit. C, 28% calcium, 31% iron

Northwest Chicken Salad `SMALL GRILL`

Perfect for an alfresco dinner on a warm evening in spring, this refreshing salad features some of the season's best produce—tender greens, fresh asparagus, and sweet strawberries.

Prep: 15 minutes **Marinate:** 10 minutes **Grill:** 4 minutes (covered) or 12 minutes (uncovered) **Serves:** 2

2 medium skinless, boneless chicken breast halves (about 8 ounces total)
1 recipe Raspberry Vinaigrette
8 to 10 asparagus spears
4 cups shredded mixed salad greens
6 to 8 strawberries
1 pear, cored and sliced
2 tablespoons chopped sweet onion
8 to 10 pecan halves, toasted (optional)

1 Place chicken in a plastic bag set in a shallow dish. Prepare Raspberry Vinaigrette; reserve half for dressing. Pour the remaining vinaigrette over chicken; seal bag. Marinate at room temperature for 10 to 15 minutes, turning bag once.

2 Lightly grease the rack of an indoor electric grill or lightly coat with cooking spray. Preheat grill. Drain chicken, discarding marinade. Place chicken on the grill rack. If using a covered grill, close lid. Grill until chicken is tender and no longer pink. (For a covered grill, allow 4 to 6 minutes. For an uncovered grill, allow 12 to 15 minutes, turning once halfway through grilling.)

3 Meanwhile, snap off and discard woody stems from asparagus spears. In a medium skillet bring a small amount of water to boiling; add asparagus. Simmer, covered, for 6 to 8 minutes or until crisp-tender; drain. To serve, divide salad greens between 2 plates. Slice chicken diagonally into bite-size strips; arrange chicken over greens. Top with asparagus, strawberries, pear, and onion. Serve with reserved vinaigrette and, if desired, pecans.

Raspberry Vinaigrette: In a screw-top jar combine ¼ cup pear nectar; 2 tablespoons salad oil; 2 tablespoons raspberry vinegar; 1 teaspoon Dijon-style mustard; 1 teaspoon toasted sesame oil; ½ to 1 teaspoon dried basil, crushed; and ⅛ teaspoon pepper. Cover and shake well. Makes about ½ cup.

Nutrition Facts per serving: 379 cal., 20 g total fat (3 g sat. fat), 59 mg chol., 131 mg sodium, 28 g carbo., 6 g fiber, 25 g pro.
Daily Values: 9% vit. A, 85% vit. C, 5% calcium, 15% iron

Turkey Steaks and Vegetables ♥

Vegetable juice—with mayo and herbs—doubles as a basting sauce for turkey steaks. Serve the savory grilled turkey and vegetables with warm Italian bread and a glass of Chianti.

Prep: 10 minutes **Grill:** 5 minutes (covered) or 9 minutes (uncovered) **Serves:** 4

Sauce

2 tablespoons vegetable juice

2 tablespoons mayonnaise or salad dressing

1½ teaspoons snipped fresh chives or green onion tops

1 teaspoon snipped fresh thyme or ½ teaspoon dried thyme, crushed

¼ teaspoon bottled minced garlic

2 ½-inch-thick turkey breast tenderloin steaks (about 8 ounces total)

1 small zucchini, halved lengthwise

2 medium plum tomatoes, halved lengthwise

1 For sauce, in a small bowl gradually stir vegetable juice into mayonnaise; stir in chives, thyme, and garlic. Set aside.

2 Lightly grease the rack of an indoor electric grill or lightly coat with cooking spray. Preheat grill. Sprinkle turkey with salt and pepper.

3 Place turkey and zucchini, cut sides down, on the grill rack. If using a covered grill, close lid. Grill until turkey is tender and no longer pink and zucchini is crisp-tender. (For a covered grill, allow 4 to 6 minutes, brushing once with sauce the last 1 minute of grilling. For an uncovered grill, allow 8 to 12 minutes, turning once halfway through and brushing occasionally with sauce the last half of grilling.) Remove from grill; cover and keep warm.

4 Add tomatoes, cut sides down, to the grill rack. If using a covered grill, close lid. Grill for 1 to 2 minutes or until tomatoes are heated through. Serve the turkey with zucchini and tomatoes.

Nutrition Facts per serving: 139 cal., 6 g total fat (1 g sat. fat), 50 mg chol., 91 mg sodium, 3 g carbo., 1 g fiber, 18 g pro.
Daily Values: 4% vit. A, 18% vit. C, 2% calcium, 7% iron

Turkey with Ginger Salsa ♥

When you're in the mood for turkey, count on these moist turkey steaks marinated in soy, sherry, and fresh ginger. Complement with this exceptional tomato-ginger salsa.

Prep: 20 minutes **Marinate:** 6 hours **Grill:** 4 minutes (covered) or 8 minutes (uncovered) **Serves:** 4

4 ½-inch-thick turkey breast
    tenderloin steaks
    (about 1 pound total)

Marinade
¼ cup vinegar
2 tablespoons dry sherry
2 tablespoons soy sauce
1 tablespoon grated fresh
    ginger
1 teaspoon crushed red
    pepper
1 clove garlic, minced

Salsa
1 medium tomato, peeled,
    seeded, and chopped
¼ cup chopped green sweet
    pepper
1 green onion, thinly sliced
1 tablespoon snipped fresh
    cilantro

4 6-inch flour tortillas

1 Place turkey in a plastic bag set in a shallow dish. For marinade, in a small bowl combine vinegar, sherry, soy sauce, ginger, crushed red pepper, and garlic. Reserve 2 tablespoons for salsa. Pour the remaining marinade over turkey; seal bag. Marinate in the refrigerator for 6 to 24 hours, turning bag occasionally.

2 Meanwhile, for salsa, in a small bowl combine tomato, sweet pepper, green onion, cilantro, and the reserved marinade. Cover and refrigerate until ready to serve. Stack tortillas and wrap in microwave-safe paper towels; set aside.

3 Lightly grease the rack of an indoor electric grill or lightly coat with cooking spray. Preheat grill. Drain turkey, discarding marinade. Place turkey on the grill rack. If using a covered grill, close lid. Grill until turkey is tender and no longer pink. (For a covered grill, allow 4 to 6 minutes. For an uncovered grill, allow 8 to 12 minutes, turning once halfway through grilling.) Microwave tortillas on 100% power (high) for 30 to 45 seconds or until warm. Serve the turkey with tortillas and salsa.

Nutrition Facts per serving: 196 cal., 4 g total fat (1 g sat. fat), 50 mg chol., 399 mg sodium, 14 g carbo., 1 g fiber, 24 g pro.
Daily Values: 4% vit. A, 18% vit. C, 3% calcium, 13% iron

Turkey-Peach Salad SMALL GRILL ♥

Fruit and poultry make a pleasing pair with a natural lightness. Here juicy turkey and a fresh peach and plum are artfully served in peach "bowls" and drizzled with a light-as-air yogurt dressing.

Prep: 25 minutes **Grill:** 4 minutes (covered) or 8 minutes (uncovered) **Serves:** 2

1 peach, pitted and cut up
1 plum, pitted and sliced
1 tablespoon lemon juice

Dressing
¼ cup lemon low-fat yogurt
1 tablespoon thinly sliced green onion
⅛ teaspoon poppy seed

2 ½-inch-thick turkey breast tenderloin steaks (about 8 ounces total)
Mixed salad greens

1 In a medium bowl combine peach and plum. Add lemon juice; toss gently to coat. For dressing, in a small bowl combine yogurt, green onion, and poppy seed. If necessary to make of drizzling consistency, stir in 1 to 2 teaspoons additional lemon juice. Set aside.

2 Lightly grease the rack of an indoor electric grill or lightly coat with cooking spray. Preheat grill. Sprinkle turkey with salt and pepper. Place turkey on the grill rack. If using a covered grill, close lid. Grill until turkey is tender and no longer pink. (For a covered grill, allow 4 to 6 minutes. For an uncovered grill, allow 8 to 12 minutes, turning once halfway through grilling.) Slice turkey diagonally into bite-size strips.

3 Divide salad greens between 2 dinner plates. (For peach bowls, see note below.) Arrange the turkey and fruit on top of greens. Drizzle with dressing.

Nutrition Facts per serving: 199 cal., 3 g total fat (1 g sat. fat), 51 mg chol., 96 mg sodium, 20 g carbo., 2 g fiber, 24 g pro.
Daily Values: 6% vit. A, 22% vit. C, 5% calcium, 7% iron

Note: To serve the salad in peach "bowls," cut 1 large peach in half crosswise; remove pit. Using a spoon, scoop out some of the pulp to create shallow "bowls." Place on top of salad greens and spoon turkey and fruit into peach halves. Drizzle with dressing.

Caesar Turkey and Penne Salad

Give an old favorite a new lease on life by adding pasta to the usual lineup of Caesar salad ingredients. There's no better way to serve this salad than with crusty French or sourdough bread.

Prep: 20 minutes **Grill:** 4 minutes (covered) or 8 minutes (uncovered) **Serves:** 4

6 ounces dried gemelli or penne pasta
4 ½-inch-thick turkey breast tenderloin steaks (about 1 pound total)
¾ cup bottled Caesar salad dressing
6 cups torn romaine lettuce
12 cherry tomatoes, halved
¼ cup finely shredded Parmesan cheese
Cracked pepper (optional)

1 Cook pasta according to package directions; drain. Meanwhile, lightly grease the rack of an indoor electric grill or lightly coat with cooking spray. Preheat grill.

2 Place turkey on the grill rack. If using a covered grill, close lid. Grill until turkey is tender and no longer pink. (For a covered grill, allow 4 to 6 minutes, brushing once with ¼ cup of the salad dressing the last 1 minute of grilling. For an uncovered grill, allow 8 to 12 minutes, turning and brushing once with ¼ cup of the salad dressing halfway through grilling.)

3 In a large salad bowl combine cooked pasta, romaine lettuce, and cherry tomatoes. Add the remaining salad dressing; toss gently to coat. Slice turkey diagonally into bite-size strips and arrange on top of greens mixture. Sprinkle with Parmesan cheese and, if desired, pepper.

Nutrition Facts per serving: 538 cal., 26 g total fat (1 g sat. fat), 55 mg chol., 138 mg sodium, 41 g carbo., 4 g fiber, 32 g pro.
Daily Values: 26% vit. A, 51% vit. C, 9% calcium, 25% iron

Fish & Seafood

Salmon with Fresh Pineapple Salsa

In this Chapter:

Sea Bass with Black Bean Relish

This island-style dish draws on the best of Cuba—the land itself (black beans, avocado, and lime) and the water that surrounds it (sea bass). Serve it with a splash of fruit juice stirred into sparkling water.

Prep: 15 minutes **Grill:** 3 minutes (covered) or 6 minutes (uncovered) **Serves:** 4

2 tablespoons snipped fresh cilantro

2 tablespoons snipped fresh oregano

½ teaspoon finely shredded lime peel

2 tablespoons lime juice

1 tablespoon olive oil

1 clove garlic, minced

¼ to ½ teaspoon bottled hot pepper sauce

1 15-ounce can black beans, rinsed and drained

1 avocado, seeded, peeled, and chopped

4 4- to 5-ounce fresh sea bass fillets, ¾ to 1 inch thick

1 In a small bowl stir together cilantro, oregano, lime peel, lime juice, oil, garlic, and pepper sauce. Transfer 2 tablespoons cilantro mixture to a medium bowl. Add beans and avocado; toss gently to coat. Cover and refrigerate until ready to serve.

2 Lightly grease the rack of an indoor electric grill or lightly coat with cooking spray. Preheat grill. Rinse fish; pat dry with paper towels. Brush both sides of fish with the remaining cilantro mixture.

3 Place fish on the grill rack, tucking under any thin edges. If using a covered grill, close lid. Grill until fish flakes easily when tested with a fork. (For a covered grill, allow 2 to 3 minutes per ½-inch thickness of fish. For an uncovered grill, allow 4 to 6 minutes per ½-inch thickness of fish, gently turning once halfway through grilling.) Serve the fish with bean mixture.

Nutrition Facts per serving: 303 cal., 15 g total fat (2 g sat. fat), 47 mg chol., 348 mg sodium, 20 g carbo., 6 g fiber, 29 g pro.
Daily Values: 9% vit. A, 16% vit. C, 4% calcium, 13% iron

Swordfish with Spicy Tomato Sauce

The best of fusion cooking comes together in this vibrant, fresh recipe. Take two popular Sicilian foods—swordfish and a spicy, fresh tomato sauce—and add them to couscous, a North African favorite.

Prep: 15 minutes **Grill:** 4 minutes (covered) or 8 minutes (uncovered) **Serves:** 4

4 5-ounce fresh swordfish
   steaks, cut 1 inch thick
4 teaspoons cooking oil
⅛ teaspoon salt
⅛ teaspoon black pepper
Sauce
¼ cup chopped onion
1 small serrano or jalapeño
   pepper, seeded and
   finely chopped
½ teaspoon ground turmeric
½ teaspoon bottled minced
   garlic
¼ teaspoon ground coriander
1½ cups chopped plum
   tomatoes
⅛ teaspoon salt
1 tablespoon snipped fresh
   cilantro

Hot cooked couscous
(optional)

1 Lightly grease the rack of an indoor electric grill or lightly coat with cooking spray. Preheat grill. Rinse fish; pat dry with paper towels. Drizzle 1 teaspoon of the oil over fish. Sprinkle with ⅛ teaspoon salt and the black pepper.

2 Place fish on the grill rack. If using a covered grill, close lid. Grill until fish flakes easily when tested with a fork. (For a covered grill, allow 4 to 6 minutes. For an uncovered grill, allow 8 to 12 minutes, gently turning once halfway through grilling.)

3 Meanwhile, for sauce, in a medium skillet heat the remaining oil. Add onion, serrano pepper, turmeric, garlic, and coriander. Cook about 2 minutes or until onion is tender. Stir in tomatoes and ⅛ teaspoon salt. Cook for 2 to 3 minutes more or just until tomatoes are softened. Remove from heat; stir in cilantro. Serve the fish with sauce and, if desired, couscous.

Nutrition Facts per serving: 237 cal., 11 g total fat (2 g sat. fat), 56 mg chol., 402 mg sodium, 5 g carbo., 1 g fiber, 29 g pro.
Daily Values: 9% vit. A, 39% vit. C, 1% calcium, 11% iron

grill fish like a pro

Testing fish for doneness can be tricky even for expert grillers. A few tips will help: Grill fish just until it is opaque through the thickest part. Don't cook it until it's dry, because it will turn tough! To be sure, poke a fork into the thickest part of the fish; gently twist the fork and pull up some of the flesh. When done, the fish will flake easily.

Maryellen Krantz
Test Kitchen Home Economist

Wasabi-Glazed Whitefish with Slaw ♥

Though its presence in this recipe is subtle, fans of fiery wasabi powder or paste—the bright-green Japanese horseradish condiment—will recognize and appreciate its head-clearing heat.

Prep: 15 minutes **Grill:** 4 minutes (covered) or 8 minutes (uncovered) **Serves:** 4

2 tablespoons light soy
    sauce

1 teaspoon toasted sesame
    oil

½ teaspoon sugar

¼ teaspoon wasabi powder
    or 1 tablespoon
    prepared horseradish

4 4-ounce fresh skinless
    whitefish, sea bass, or
    orange roughy fillets,
    1 inch thick

Slaw

1 medium zucchini,
    coarsely shredded
    (about 1⅓ cups)

1 cup sliced radishes

1 cup fresh pea pods

2 tablespoons snipped fresh
    chives

3 tablespoons rice vinegar

1 Lightly grease the rack of an indoor electric grill or lightly coat with cooking spray. Preheat grill. In a small bowl combine soy sauce, ½ teaspoon of the sesame oil, ¼ teaspoon of the sugar, and the wasabi powder. Rinse fish; pat dry with paper towels. Brush both sides of fish with soy mixture.

2 Place fish on the grill rack, tucking under any thin edges. If using a covered grill, close lid. Grill until fish flakes easily when tested with a fork. (For a covered grill, allow 4 to 6 minutes. For an uncovered grill, allow 8 to 12 minutes, gently turning once halfway through grilling.)

3 Meanwhile, for slaw, in a medium bowl combine zucchini, radishes, pea pods, and chives. Stir together vinegar, the remaining sesame oil, and the remaining sugar. Drizzle over zucchini mixture; toss to combine. Serve the fish with slaw.

Nutrition Facts per serving: 141 cal., 3 g total fat (1 g sat. fat), 60 mg chol., 363 mg sodium, 6 g carbo., 1 g fiber, 24 g pro.
Daily Values: 3% vit. A, 46% vit. C, 3% calcium, 10% iron

Greek Swordfish with Lemon Orzo

A Greek-style cucumber-yogurt sauce tops this grilled swordfish. Just one taste will transport you to a romantic taverna table in the Plaka, the old-town district in Athens.

Prep: 20 minutes **Grill:** 4 minutes (covered) or 8 minutes (uncovered) **Serves:** 4

4   4-ounce fresh or frozen swordfish steaks, cut 1 inch thick

½   of a small cucumber, peeled, halved lengthwise, and seeded

½   cup plain fat-free yogurt

1   tablespoon walnut pieces

1   teaspoon olive oil

1   clove garlic, minced

1½ teaspoons snipped fresh dill

1   cup dried orzo pasta (rosamarina)

¼   cup crumbled feta cheese (1 ounce)

1   tablespoon olive oil

1   tablespoon lemon juice

1   tablespoon olive oil

½   teaspoon salt

¼   teaspoon freshly ground pepper

1 Thaw fish, if frozen. For sauce, coarsely chop half of the cucumber; finely chop the remaining cucumber.

2 In a food processor bowl or blender container combine coarsely chopped cucumber, 2 tablespoons of the yogurt, the walnuts, the 1 teaspoon oil, and garlic. Cover and process or blend until smooth. Transfer to a small bowl; stir in finely chopped cucumber, remaining yogurt, and dill.

3 Cook pasta according to package directions; drain. Return pasta to saucepan. Add feta cheese, 1 tablespoon oil, and lemon juice; toss to coat. Season to taste with salt and pepper.

4 Meanwhile, lightly grease the rack of an indoor electric grill or lightly coat with cooking spray. Preheat grill. Rinse fish; pat dry with paper towels. Brush with 1 tablespoon oil; sprinkle with the ½ teaspoon salt and the ¼ teaspoon pepper.

5 Place fish on the grill rack. If using a covered grill, close lid. Grill until fish flakes easily when tested with a fork. (For a covered grill, allow 4 to 6 minutes. For an uncovered grill, allow 8 to 12 minutes, gently turning once halfway through grilling.) To serve, spoon the sauce over fish. Serve with pasta mixture.

Nutrition Facts per serving: 379 cal., 17 g total fat (5 g sat. fat), 59 mg chol., 637 mg sodium, 24 g carbo., 0 g fiber, 30 g pro.
Daily Values: 5% vit. A, 7% vit. C, 12% calcium, 15% iron

Salmon with Fresh Pineapple Salsa ♥

You don't need to have a party to enjoy the sweet-hot fruit salsa that's as pretty as a sprinkling of confetti on top of this grilled salmon. Serve it with hot cooked rice any night of the week.

Prep: 25 minutes **Grill:** 4 minutes (covered) or 8 minutes (uncovered) **Serves:** 4

Salsa

- 2 cups coarsely chopped fresh pineapple
- ½ cup chopped red sweet pepper
- ¼ cup finely chopped red onion
- 3 tablespoons lime juice
- 1 tablespoon snipped fresh cilantro or chives
- 1 tablespoon honey
- 1 small fresh jalapeño pepper, seeded and finely chopped

- 1 1-pound fresh skinless salmon fillet, 1 inch thick
- ¼ teaspoon ground cumin

1 For salsa, in a medium bowl combine pineapple, sweet pepper, onion, 2 tablespoons of the lime juice, the cilantro, honey, and jalapeño pepper. Cover and refrigerate up to 2 hours.

2 Lightly grease the rack of an indoor electric grill or lightly coat with cooking spray. Preheat grill. Rinse fish; pat dry with paper towels. Cut into 4 serving-size pieces. Brush both sides of fish with the remaining lime juice and sprinkle with cumin.

3 Place fish on the grill rack, tucking under any thin edges. If using a covered grill, close lid. Grill until fish flakes easily when tested with a fork. (For a covered grill, allow 4 to 6 minutes. For an uncovered grill, allow 8 to 12 minutes, gently turning once halfway through grilling.) Serve the fish with salsa.

Nutrition Facts per serving: 170 cal., 4 g total fat (1 g sat. fat), 20 mg chol., 70 mg sodium, 17 g carbo., 1 g fiber, 17 g pro.
Daily Values: 16% vit. A, 75% vit. C, 1% calcium, 9% iron

Panzanella with Grilled Tuna SMALL GRILL

"Pane" means bread in Italian, and making panzanella, a sensational salad, is a wonderful way to make good use of bread that's not as fresh as just-baked, but still too good to throw away.

Prep: 20 minutes   **Grill:** 2 minutes (covered) or 4 minutes (uncovered)   **Stand:** 5 minutes   **Serves:** 2

Sauce

- ¼ cup bottled balsamic vinaigrette or red wine vinegar salad dressing
- ¼ teaspoon finely snipped fresh rosemary

- 8 ounces fresh tuna steaks, cut ½ to 1 inch thick
- 1 cup torn mixed salad greens
- ¾ cup broccoli flowerets
- 1 small tomato, chopped
- 2 tablespoons thinly sliced green onion
- 2 cups 1-inch cubes day-old Italian bread
- Finely shredded Parmesan cheese (optional)

1 Lightly grease the rack of an indoor electric grill or lightly coat with cooking spray. Preheat grill. For sauce, in a small bowl combine vinaigrette and rosemary. Reserve 2 tablespoons for dressing.

2 Rinse fish; pat dry with paper towels. Place fish on the grill rack. If using a covered grill, close lid. Grill until fish flakes easily when tested with a fork. (For a covered grill, allow 2 to 3 minutes per ½-inch thickness of fish, brushing once with remaining sauce the last 1 minute of grilling. For an uncovered grill, allow 4 to 6 minutes per ½-inch thickness of fish, gently turning and brushing once with remaining sauce halfway through grilling.)

3 Meanwhile, in a large salad bowl combine greens, broccoli, tomato, and green onion. Flake fish; add to greens mixture. Drizzle with the reserved sauce; toss gently to coat. Add bread cubes; toss gently to combine. Let stand for 5 minutes before serving. If desired, sprinkle with cheese.

Nutrition Facts per serving: 380 cal., 17 g total fat (3 g sat. fat), 47 mg chol., 608 mg sodium, 24 g carbo., 2 g fiber, 33 g pro.
Daily Values: 82% vit. A, 69% vit. C, 5% calcium, 19% iron

choosing the best skewers

Kabobs are one of my family's favorite meals, and I've found that they're easier to make than ever on an indoor grill. To get the most food on the grill at once, I use 6-inch bamboo skewers. I prefer this kind because they allow me to close the lid on my covered grill. You also can use metal ones, but the handles take up more space, so you might not be able to fit as many kabobs on your grill.

Marilyn Cornelius
Test Kitchen Home Economist

Rosemary-Orange Shrimp Kabobs

Bacon-wrapped shrimp sounds decadent, but it can be everyday fare if you use light turkey bacon. The subtle smokiness from the bacon combines with a pleasing sweetness from brushed-on herbed orange juice.

Prep: 20 minutes **Grill:** 2½ minutes (covered) or 6 minutes (uncovered) **Serves:** 2

8 ounces fresh large shrimp in shells (about 10)
5 slices turkey bacon, halved crosswise
¾ cup red, yellow, and/or green sweet pepper cut into 1-inch pieces
1½ teaspoons finely shredded orange or blood orange peel
1 tablespoon orange or blood orange juice
1 teaspoon snipped fresh rosemary
1½ cups hot cooked rice
¾ cup cooked or canned black beans, rinsed and drained

1 Peel and devein shrimp, leaving tails intact. Rinse shrimp; pat dry with paper towels. Wrap each shrimp in a half slice of bacon. On 6-inch skewers, alternately thread shrimp and sweet pepper pieces. In a small bowl combine ½ teaspoon of the orange peel, the orange juice, and rosemary. Brush over kabobs.

2 Meanwhile, lightly grease the rack of an indoor electric grill or lightly coat with cooking spray. Preheat grill. Place kabobs on the grill rack. If using a covered grill, close lid. Grill until shrimp turn pink and bacon is crisp. (For a covered grill, allow 2½ to 4 minutes. For an uncovered grill, allow 6 to 8 minutes, turning occasionally to cook evenly.)

3 In a medium saucepan stir together the cooked rice, beans, and remaining orange peel; heat through. Serve the shrimp and pepper skewers with rice mixture.

Nutrition Facts per serving: 434 cal., 8 g total fat (2 g sat. fat), 154 mg chol., 865 mg sodium, 60 g carbo., 7 g fiber, 33 g pro.
Daily Values: 37% vit. A, 190% vit. C, 9% calcium, 31% iron

Scallop Brochettes ♥

A little bit sweet, a little bit tangy, these seafood brochettes—soaked in a simple marinade of sherry, mustard, honey, and soy sauce—can be made with scallops, shrimp, or a combination of both.

Prep: 15 minutes **Marinate:** 30 minutes **Grill:** 2½ minutes (covered) or 6 minutes (uncovered) **Serves:** 4

1 pound fresh sea scallops
　　and/or peeled and
　　deveined large shrimp
Marinade
2 tablespoons cooking oil
2 tablespoons dry sherry
2 tablespoons stone-ground
　　mustard
1 tablespoon honey
1½ teaspoons soy sauce

1 Rinse scallops; pat dry with paper towels. Halve large scallops (you should have about 20 pieces). Place scallops in a plastic bag set in a shallow dish. For marinade, in a small bowl combine oil, sherry, mustard, honey, and soy sauce. Pour over scallops; seal bag. Marinate in the refrigerator for 30 minutes, turning bag occasionally.

2 Lightly grease the rack of an indoor electric grill or lightly coat with cooking spray. Preheat grill. Drain scallops, discarding marinade. On 6-inch skewers, thread scallops. (If using both scallops and shrimp, thread a scallop in the "curl" of each shrimp.)

3 Place kabobs on the grill rack. If using a covered grill, close lid. Grill until scallops are opaque. (For a covered grill, allow 2½ to 4 minutes. For an uncovered grill, allow 6 to 8 minutes, turning occasionally to cook evenly.)

Nutrition Facts per serving: 119 cal., 5 g total fat (1 g sat. fat), 34 mg chol., 284 mg sodium, 4 g carbo., 0 g fiber, 15 g pro.
Daily Values: 0% vit. A, 0% vit. C, 6% calcium, 13% iron

sea scallop know-how

Sea scallops are the largest variety of scallops and the easiest to grill. When you purchase them, they should be firm, sweet smelling, and free of excess cloudy liquid. For best flavor, refrigerate the shucked scallops covered with their own liquid in a closed container for no longer than 2 days.

Vegetables

Grilled Vegetable Salad

In this Chapter:

Asparagus with Sorrel Dressing SMALL GRILL

The taste of lemon brings out the very best in fresh asparagus. Here the lemony tartness comes from delicate sorrel greens, which are used to flavor the herb-infused yogurt-mayonnaise dressing.

Prep: 15 minutes   **Grill:** 2 minutes (covered) or 3 minutes (uncovered)   **Serves:** 2

Dressing

- 2 tablespoons plain low-fat yogurt
- 2 tablespoons mayonnaise or salad dressing
- 2 tablespoons finely snipped sorrel or spinach
- 1 small green onion, thinly sliced
- ½ teaspoon lemon-pepper seasoning (optional)

- 8 ounces asparagus spears

1 For dressing, in a small bowl combine yogurt, mayonnaise, sorrel, green onion, and, if desired, lemon-pepper seasoning. Cover and refrigerate until ready to serve.

2 Snap off and discard woody stems from asparagus spears. In a medium skillet bring a small amount of water to boiling; add asparagus. Simmer, covered, for 3 minutes; drain.

3 Lightly grease the rack of an indoor electric grill or lightly coat with cooking spray. Preheat grill. Place asparagus on the grill rack. If using a covered grill, close lid. Grill until asparagus is crisp-tender and light brown. (For a covered grill, allow 2 to 4 minutes. For an uncovered grill, allow 3 to 5 minutes, turning occasionally to cook evenly.) Serve the asparagus with dressing.

Nutrition Facts per serving: 129 cal., 11 g total fat (2 g sat. fat), 9 mg chol., 95 mg sodium, 5 g carbo., 2 g fiber, 3 g pro.
Daily Values: 10% vit. A, 38% vit. C, 4% calcium, 5% iron

veggie grilling tips

Fresh vegetables taste great when they're grilled. Here are some pointers for grilling them to perfection:

● If you grill vegetables using skewers, don't crowd the vegetables; leave a small space (about ¼ inch) between pieces to ensure even cooking.

● Since they require different grilling times, you'll want to avoid pairing large hunks of meat with quick-cooking vegetables. Instead make separate skewers for each type of vegetable and for the meat so each can be removed from the grill when it's done.

● Cut the vegetables into uniform sizes and shapes so they will cook evenly.

● Bonus tip: Besides enjoying roasted vegetables warm off the grill, you can use the leftovers in a variety of ways. Stir vegetable pieces or strips into pasta sauce, add them to soups or pizza, stir a few into rice pilaf, or roll them up in tortillas.

Ratatouille on a Skewer

The mild, sweet taste and meaty texture of eggplant lends itself especially well to grilling. This lovely combination of vibrant vegetables is the perfect accompaniment to steaks or chops.

Prep: 20 minutes **Grill:** 4 minutes (covered) or 8 minutes (uncovered) **Serves:** 4

½ of a medium eggplant, peeled and cut into 1-inch cubes (about 3 cups)

1 medium zucchini, halved lengthwise and sliced 1 inch thick

½ cup green and/or yellow sweet pepper cut into 1-inch pieces

1 small onion, cut into wedges

¼ cup bottled French salad dressing

3 tablespoons grated Parmesan cheese

3 tablespoons fine dry bread crumbs

8 cherry tomatoes

1 Preheat indoor electric grill. On eight 6-inch skewers, alternately thread eggplant, zucchini, sweet pepper, and onion, leaving ¼ inch between pieces. Brush with salad dressing. Combine the Parmesan cheese and bread crumbs; place on a piece of waxed paper. Roll the kabobs in the crumb mixture to coat evenly.

2 Place kabobs on the grill rack. If using a covered grill, close lid. Grill until zucchini is crisp-tender. (For a covered grill, allow 4 to 5 minutes, giving kabobs a quarter turn once halfway through and placing tomatoes on ends of skewers the last 1 minute of grilling. For an uncovered grill, allow 8 to 10 minutes, turning occasionally to cook evenly and placing tomatoes on ends of skewers the last 2 minutes of grilling.)

Nutrition Facts per serving: 146 cal., 8 g total fat (2 g sat. fat), 3 mg chol., 330 mg sodium, 16 g carbo., 3 g fiber, 4 g pro.
Daily Values: 8% vit. A, 49% vit. C, 8% calcium, 6% iron

Summer Squash with Cheese & Sage

The smaller the squash, the sweeter they are likely to be. As the squash cook, their natural sugar caramelizes, giving them a nutty, rich flavor—terrific company for the salty tang of goat cheese.

Prep: 5 minutes **Grill:** 3 minutes (covered) or 5 minutes (uncovered) **Serves:** 4

1 pound small yellow summer squash or zucchini
1 teaspoon olive oil
¼ cup mild picante sauce
2 tablespoons crumbled chèvre (goat cheese) or shredded Monterey Jack cheese
1 tablespoon snipped fresh sage, oregano, or cilantro

1 Preheat indoor electric grill. Trim ends from squash; halve squash lengthwise. Brush squash with oil.

2 Place squash on the grill rack. If using a covered grill, close lid. Grill until squash are crisp-tender. (For a covered grill, allow about 3 minutes, brushing once with picante sauce halfway through grilling. For an uncovered grill, allow 5 to 6 minutes, turning once halfway through grilling and brushing occasionally with picante sauce.)

3 Transfer grilled squash to a serving dish and sprinkle with the cheese and fresh sage.

Nutrition Facts per serving: 54 cal., 4 g total fat (1 g sat. fat), 7 mg chol., 156 mg sodium, 5 g carbo., 1 g fiber, 2 g pro.
Daily Values: 4% vit. A, 14% vit. C, 1% calcium, 3% iron

fresh-herb interchanges

Fresh herbs turn ordinary dishes into extraordinary ones. Herbs each have their own distinct flavors, but that doesn't mean you can't replace one for another. Try these substitutions:

- Sage: use savory, marjoram, or rosemary

- Basil: substitute oregano or thyme

- Thyme: basil, marjoram, oregano, or savory will suffice

- Mint: substitute basil, marjoram, or rosemary

- Rosemary: try thyme, tarragon, or savory

- Cilantro: substitute parsley

Piquant Grilled Broccoli & Olives

Broccoli on the grill? You bet! This intensely flavored side dish makes a great partner for any grilled or broiled meat or poultry—or, toss it with hot cooked pasta for a vegetarian entrée.

Prep: 15 minutes **Marinate:** 10 minutes **Grill:** 3 minutes (covered) or 6 minutes (uncovered) **Serves:** 4

3½ cups broccoli flowerets
½ cup pitted ripe olives
Marinade
  ½ of a 2-ounce can anchovy
      fillets, drained and
      finely chopped
      (optional)
  2 tablespoons snipped
      fresh oregano or Italian
      flat-leaf parsley
  2 tablespoons red wine
      vinegar
  2 tablespoons olive oil
  5 cloves garlic, minced
  ¼ teaspoon crushed red
      pepper
      Dash salt

1 In a large saucepan bring a small amount of water to boiling; add broccoli. Simmer, covered, for 2 minutes; drain. In a medium bowl combine broccoli and olives. For marinade, in a small bowl whisk together anchovies (if desired), oregano, vinegar, oil, garlic, red pepper, and salt. Pour over broccoli and olives; toss to coat. Marinate at room temperature for 10 minutes, stirring occasionally.

2 Meanwhile, lightly grease the rack of an indoor electric grill or lightly coat with cooking spray. Preheat grill. Drain broccoli and olives, discarding marinade. On 6-inch skewers, alternately thread broccoli and olives, leaving ¼ inch between pieces.

3 Place kabobs on the grill rack. If using a covered grill, close lid. Grill until broccoli is light brown and tender. (For a covered grill, allow 3 to 4 minutes, giving kabobs a quarter turn once halfway through grilling. For an uncovered grill, allow 6 to 8 minutes, turning occasionally to cook evenly.) Remove broccoli and olives from skewers.

Nutrition Facts per serving: 91 cal., 8 g total fat (1 g sat. fat), 0 mg chol., 125 mg sodium, 6 g carbo., 3 g fiber, 3 g pro.
Daily Values: 13% vit. A, 121% vit. C, 4% calcium, 6% iron

Grilled Vegetable Salad

These sparkling grilled vegetables are the essence of simplicity—a drizzle of balsamic vinegar and a sprinkle of fresh basil is their only embellishment.

Prep: 20 minutes **Grill:** 4 minutes (covered) or 8 minutes (uncovered) **Serves:** 4 to 6

1 small eggplant, cut crosswise into 1-inch slices

12 thin asparagus spears

2 medium red sweet peppers, cut into ¾-inch rings

1 small red onion, cut into ¾-inch slices

1 small zucchini, sliced lengthwise into ¼-inch slices

1 small yellow summer squash, sliced lengthwise into ¼-inch slices

2 tablespoons olive oil

4 cups torn mixed salad greens

3 tablespoons balsamic vinegar

3 tablespoons shredded fresh basil

1 Preheat indoor electric grill. Brush vegetables with olive oil and, if desired, sprinkle with salt and freshly ground black pepper. Divide salad greens among 4 to 6 salad plates. Set aside.

2 Place vegetables on the grill rack. (If necessary, cook vegetables in batches.) If using a covered grill, close lid. Grill until vegetables are crisp-tender. (For a covered grill, allow 4 to 5 minutes. For an uncovered grill, allow 8 to 10 minutes for eggplant, sweet peppers, and onion, and 5 to 6 minutes for asparagus, zucchini, and yellow squash, turning occasionally to cook evenly.)

3 Separate onion slices into rings. If desired, cut vegetables into bite-size pieces. Arrange vegetables on top of salad greens. Drizzle with vinegar and sprinkle with basil.

Nutrition Facts per serving: 141 cal., 7 g total fat (1 g sat. fat), 0 mg chol., 16 mg sodium, 17 g carbo., 6 g fiber, 3 g pro.
Daily Values: 37% vit. A, 204% vit. C, 4% calcium, 8% iron

Sauces, Marinades, & Rubs

Honey-Peach Sauce

In this Chapter:

Tomato-Molasses-Mustard Sauce

Consider this sauce a true melting pot of flavor. Its multiregional echoes promise to satisfy purists from all parts of the country.

Prep: 10 minutes **Cook:** 10 minutes **Serves:** 16

¼ cup finely chopped onion
6 cloves garlic, minced
½ teaspoon paprika
¼ to ½ teaspoon crushed red pepper
1 tablespoon cooking oil
1 15-ounce can tomato puree
3 tablespoons cider vinegar
3 tablespoons molasses
2 tablespoons brown sugar
2 tablespoons stone-ground mustard
½ teaspoon salt
½ teaspoon dried oregano, crushed
½ teaspoon liquid smoke (optional)

1 In a medium saucepan cook onion, garlic, paprika, and crushed red pepper in hot oil over medium heat until onion is tender.

2 Stir in the tomato puree, vinegar, molasses, brown sugar, mustard, salt, oregano, and, if desired, liquid smoke. Bring to boiling; reduce heat. Simmer, uncovered, about 10 minutes or until sauce is thickened, stirring frequently.

3 Grill beef, pork, or boneless poultry according to the chart on the inside front cover, brushing once with some of the sauce the last 2 to 3 minutes on a covered grill or brushing occasionally the last half of grilling on an uncovered grill. If desired, reheat and pass additional sauce.

Nutrition Facts per 2 tablespoons: 38 cal., 2 g total fat (0 g sat. fat), 0 mg chol., 200 mg sodium, 8 g carbo., 0 g fiber, 0 g pro.
Daily Values: 4% vit. A, 16% vit. C, 0% calcium, 2% iron

Note: This sauce can be frozen in small freezer containers for use at other times. Thaw in the refrigerator overnight.

Peanut Saté Sauce

When the mood strikes for something on the exotic side, stir up this rich saté sauce with Thai overtones. It's particularly fitting paired with succulent grilled chicken.

Prep: 10 minutes **Serves:** 8

¼ cup creamy peanut butter
2 tablespoons rice vinegar or white vinegar
2 tablespoons soy sauce
1 teaspoon bottled minced garlic
½ teaspoon toasted sesame oil
⅛ teaspoon crushed red pepper
2 tablespoons thinly sliced green onion

1 In a small bowl stir together the peanut butter, vinegar, soy sauce, garlic, sesame oil, and red pepper. Stir in green onion.

2 Grill boneless poultry, meat, or fish according to the chart on the inside front cover, brushing once with some of the sauce the last 1 to 2 minutes on a covered grill or brushing occasionally the last half of grilling on an uncovered grill. If desired, reheat and pass any remaining sauce.

Nutrition Facts per tablespoon: 56 cal., 4 g total fat (1 g sat. fat), 0 mg chol., 268 mg sodium, 2 g carbo., 1 g fiber, 3 g pro.
Daily Values: 0% vit. A, 1% vit. C, 1% calcium, 1% iron

ready, set, clean

Love to grill, but hate to clean up? Well, here's some good news—indoor grills are designed to keep dishwashing chores to a minimum.

● Start by reading and following the manufacturer's directions for your grill.

● After grilling, unplug your grill and let it cool to the point that you can touch it safely. To loosen stubborn food, lay wet paper towels over the grill rack and let it soak.

To clean *covered* grills:
● Never immerse a covered grill in water. Some grills have a grill rack that can be removed.

● Wipe a nonremovable grill rack with a warm, damp paper towel or sponge. A bit of dishwashing detergent helps get the job done.

● Wash a removable grill rack and the drip pan in hot, soapy water, then rinse and dry.

To clean *uncovered* grills:
● For easier cleanup, line the drip pan or base with foil or coat with cooking spray before grilling.

● Remove the power cord or heat control, then wash the grill rack and drip pan in hot, soapy water; rinse and dry. Or, wash the rack and pan in the dishwasher, if recommended.

Honey-Peach Sauce

This sweet barbecue sauce is the taste of summer boiled down to the basics: juicy peaches, honey, zingy cracked black pepper, and fresh thyme.

Prep: 10 minutes **Cook:** 15 minutes **Serves:** 8 to 12

4   medium peaches
        (about 1⅓ pounds)
2   tablespoons lemon juice
2   tablespoons honey
½   teaspoon cracked pepper
1   to 2 teaspoons snipped
        fresh thyme

1 Peel and cut up 3 of the peaches. Place in a blender container or food processor bowl. Add lemon juice, honey, and pepper. Cover and blend or process until smooth. Transfer to a medium saucepan.

2 Bring to boiling; reduce heat. Simmer, uncovered, about 15 minutes or until sauce is slightly thickened, stirring occasionally. Remove from heat. Finely chop the remaining peach; stir into the sauce. Stir in thyme.

3 Grill meat, boneless poultry, or fish according to the chart on the inside front cover. Serve with the sauce.

Nutrition Facts per 3 tablespoons: 50 cal., 0 g total fat (0 g sat. fat), 0 mg chol.,
0 mg sodium, 13 g carbo., 2 g fiber, 1 g pro.
Daily Values: 4% vit. A, 12% vit. C, 1% calcium, 1% iron

Beer-Mustard Marinade

This German-style marinade brings pork chops and fresh bratwurst to a new level. Prick the sausages first to let the flavors penetrate. Serve with deli coleslaw or pasta salad.

Prep: 10 minutes **Marinate:** 8 hours **Yield:** about 1½ cups (enough for 3 to 3½ pounds meat)

1   cup beer or nonalcoholic beer
¼   cup Dijon-style mustard or stone-ground mustard
3   tablespoons mild-flavored molasses
2   teaspoons white wine Worcestershire sauce
½   teaspoon ground nutmeg
¼   teaspoon ground cloves

1 In a small bowl combine beer, mustard, molasses, Worcestershire sauce, nutmeg, and cloves. Pour marinade over pork, beef, or lamb in a plastic bag set in a shallow dish; seal bag.

2 Marinate in the refrigerator for 8 to 24 hours, turning bag occasionally. Drain, discarding marinade.

3 Grill the pork, beef, or lamb according to the chart on the inside front cover.

Nutrition Facts per tablespoon: 7 cal., 0 g total fat (0 g sat. fat), 0 mg chol., 10 mg sodium, 1 g carbo., 0 g fiber, 0 g pro.
Daily Values: 0% vit. A, 0% vit. C, 1% calcium, 1% iron

Soy-Citrus Marinade

The mix of citrus, soy, garlic, and brown sugar adds pizzazz to this Asian-accented marinade. Don't exceed the marinating time for seafood or fish—the acid can "cook" the seafood, making it inedible.

Prep: 10 minutes **Marinate:** 1 hour **Yield:** about ¾ cup (enough for about 2 pounds seafood, fish, or poultry)

¼   cup soy sauce
1   tablespoon finely shredded orange peel
¼   cup orange juice
1   tablespoon finely shredded lemon peel
3   tablespoons lemon juice
1   tablespoon brown sugar
2   teaspoons toasted sesame oil
3   cloves garlic, minced

1 In a small bowl combine soy sauce, orange peel, orange juice, lemon peel, lemon juice, brown sugar, sesame oil, and garlic. Stir until the sugar is dissolved.

2 Pour marinade over seafood, fish, or boneless poultry in a plastic bag set in a shallow dish; seal bag. Marinate in the refrigerator for 1 to 2 hours, turning bag occasionally. Drain, discarding marinade.

3 Grill the seafood, fish, or poultry according to the chart on the inside front cover.

Nutrition Facts per tablespoon: 9 cal., 0 g total fat (0 g sat. fat), 0 mg chol., 154 mg sodium, 1 g carbo., 0 g fiber, 0 g pro.
Daily Values: 0% vit. A, 5% vit. C, 0% calcium, 0% iron

Herb Rub

Here's an aromatic way to flavor grilled meats that doesn't depend on having fresh herbs. If your dried seasonings haven't been called into service during the past year, pitch 'em and buy new ones.

Prep: 5 minutes   **Yield:** about 2 teaspoons, enough for about 1½ pounds meat, poultry, or fish (6 servings)

½ teaspoon salt
½ teaspoon dried thyme, crushed
½ teaspoon dried rosemary, crushed
½ teaspoon dried savory, crushed
¼ teaspoon pepper

1 In a small bowl combine salt, thyme, rosemary, savory, and pepper. Sprinkle the mixture evenly over meat, boneless poultry, or fish; rub in with your fingers.

2 Grill the meat, poultry, or fish according to the chart on the inside front cover.

Nutrition Facts per serving: 3 cal., 0 g total fat (0 g sat. fat), 0 mg chol., 194 mg sodium, 0 g carbo., 0 g fiber, 0 g pro.
Daily Values: 0% vit. A, 0% vit. C, 0% calcium, 1% iron

Sweet and Spicy Rub

Turn your backyard into a mecca for meat lovers with this Middle Eastern rub. Its flavors are particularly good paired with lamb chops, steaks, and chicken.

Prep: 10 minutes   **Yield:** about ¼ cup, enough for about 3 pounds meat or poultry (12 servings)

2 tablespoons margarine or butter
1 teaspoon ground cinnamon
½ teaspoon salt
½ teaspoon ground cumin
½ teaspoon ground turmeric
½ teaspoon ground red pepper
½ teaspoon black pepper
¼ teaspoon ground cardamom
⅛ teaspoon ground cloves
⅛ teaspoon ground nutmeg
1 tablespoon sugar

1 In a small saucepan melt margarine. Stir in cinnamon, salt, cumin, turmeric, red pepper, black pepper, cardamom, cloves, and nutmeg. Remove from heat. Stir in sugar; cool.

2 Sprinkle the mixture evenly over meat or boneless poultry; rub in with your fingers.

3 Grill the meat or poultry according to the chart on the inside front cover.

Nutrition Facts per serving: 23 cal., 2 g total fat (0 g sat. fat), 0 mg chol., 119 mg sodium, 1 g carbo., 0 g fiber, 0 g pro.
Daily Values: 2% vit. A, 0% vit. C, 0% calcium, 1% iron

Cooking
for Friends

Spicy Chicken & Star Fruit

In this Chapter:

Portobellos with Avocado Salsa

Get the party off to a sassy start. Toss portobello mushrooms on the grill and top with salsa for a rich, meaty flavor that will seduce even the most avid meat lover.

Prep: 20 minutes **Grill:** 3 minutes (covered) or 6 minutes (uncovered) **Serves:** 8

4   6- to 8-ounce fresh
    portobello mushrooms
3   tablespoons balsamic
    vinegar
2   tablespoons red wine
    vinegar
2   tablespoons olive oil
¼   teaspoon crushed red
    pepper

Salsa

1   medium avocado, seeded,
    peeled, and chopped
1   medium tomato, chopped
¼   cup sliced green onions
¼   cup crumbled, crisp-
    cooked bacon
2   tablespoons snipped fresh
    cilantro

1 Preheat indoor electric grill. Cut off mushroom stems even with caps; discard stems. In a small bowl combine vinegars, olive oil, and red pepper. Reserve ¼ cup for salsa.

2 Place mushroom caps on the grill rack. If using a covered grill, close lid. Grill until mushrooms are tender. (For a covered grill, allow 3 to 4 minutes, brushing once with remaining vinegar mixture halfway through grilling. For an uncovered grill, allow 6 to 8 minutes, turning and brushing once with remaining vinegar mixture halfway through grilling.)

3 For salsa, in a medium bowl combine avocado, tomato, green onions, bacon, cilantro, and the reserved vinegar mixture. Cut the mushrooms into ½-inch slices. Spoon the salsa over mushroom slices.

Nutrition Facts per serving: 117 cal., 8 g total fat (2 g sat. fat), 2 mg chol., 44 mg sodium, 10 g carbo., 2 g fiber, 3 g pro.
Daily Values: 4% vit. A, 18% vit. C, 0% calcium, 13% iron

Mexican Pitas with Tropical Salsa

These cheesy quesadilla appetizers are the essence of much-loved Mexican food! Look for American-made Mexican cheeses in your supermarket—they're known for their superior melting quality.

Prep: 25 minutes **Grill:** 4 minutes (covered) or 8 minutes (uncovered) **Serves:** 8

Salsa
- ½ cup finely chopped fresh mango
- ½ cup finely chopped fresh pineapple
- ¼ cup finely chopped red onion
- 2 tablespoons snipped fresh cilantro
- 1 tablespoon lime juice
- 1 small fresh red serrano pepper, seeded and finely chopped

- 4 large pita bread rounds, halved crosswise
- 1½ cups shredded asadero, Chihuahua, or Monterey Jack cheese (6 ounces)
- 4 teaspoons olive oil

1 For salsa, in a medium bowl combine mango, pineapple, red onion, cilantro, lime juice, and serrano pepper. Cover and refrigerate up to 2 hours.

2 Preheat indoor electric grill. Fill pita bread halves with shredded cheese. Gently press each pita half to flatten and seal slightly. Brush the outsides of the pita halves with olive oil.

3 Place pitas on the grill rack. If using a covered grill, close lid. Grill until cheese is melted and bread is slightly crisp. (For a covered grill, allow about 4 minutes. For an uncovered grill, allow 8 to 10 minutes, turning once halfway through grilling.)

4 To serve, place pita halves on a serving platter or individual plates. Pass salsa, to be scooped up with torn pieces of pita.

Nutrition Facts per serving: 179 cal., 7 g total fat (3 g sat. fat), 19 mg chol., 372 mg sodium, 21 g carbo., 1 g fiber, 8 g pro.
Daily Values: 7% vit. A, 14% vit. C, 9% calcium, 5% iron

appetizing ideas

Even for the most casual get-togethers, it's nice to have an assortment of nibbles for your guests to enjoy as a prelude to the main event. When I'm planning a no-fuss evening, I make one simple starter from scratch. Then I fill in with purchased crudités, bagel chips, tortilla chips with salsa, purchased hummus with warm wedges of pita bread, or marinated olives. Stylish but easy!

Kay Springer
Test Kitchen Home Economist

Mahi Mahi with Vegetable Slaw ♥

Tongue-tingling, but far from fierce, the marinade used for these fish fillets has a hint of honey that makes for a perfect balance of sweet and heat.

Prep: 15 minutes **Marinate:** 30 minutes **Grill:** 2 minutes (covered) or 4 minutes (uncovered) **Serves:** 6

6 5- to 6-ounce fresh or frozen mahi mahi or pike fillets, ½ to ¾ inch thick

Marinade
⅓ cup snipped fresh cilantro
1½ teaspoons finely shredded lime peel (set aside)
⅓ cup lime juice
¼ cup olive oil
4 teaspoons honey
1 fresh jalapeño pepper, seeded and finely chopped
4 cloves garlic, minced
¼ teaspoon salt

Slaw
2¼ cups packaged shredded cabbage with carrot (coleslaw mix)
1½ cups shredded jicama

Grilled lemon or lime slices (optional)

1 Thaw fish, if frozen. Rinse fish; pat dry with paper towels. Place fish in a shallow dish. For marinade, in a small bowl combine cilantro, lime juice, oil, honey, jalapeño pepper, garlic, and salt; divide in half. Stir lime peel into one portion of marinade and pour over fish; turn fish to coat. Cover and marinate at room temperature for 30 minutes. Reserve the remaining marinade for dressing.

2 For slaw, in a medium bowl combine cabbage and jicama. Pour the reserved marinade over cabbage mixture; toss to coat. Cover and refrigerate until ready to serve.

3 Lightly grease the rack of an indoor electric grill or lightly coat with cooking spray. Preheat grill. Drain fish, discarding marinade. Place fish on the grill rack, tucking under any thin edges. If using a covered grill, close lid.

4 Grill until fish flakes easily when tested with a fork. (For a covered grill, allow 2 to 3 minutes per ½-inch thickness of fish. For an uncovered grill, allow 4 to 6 minutes per ½-inch thickness of fish, gently turning once halfway through grilling.) Serve the fish with slaw. If desired, garnish with lemon slices.

Nutrition Facts per serving: 247 cal., 10 g total fat (1 g sat. fat), 103 mg chol., 231 mg sodium, 12 g carbo., 1 g fiber, 27 g pro.
Daily Values: 24% vit. A, 39% vit. C, 4% calcium, 12% iron

Shrimp and Papaya Salad

Who could resist this salad? Curried honey and yogurt dressing spiffs up tropical papayas, colorful and crisp sweet peppers, and best of all, the special treat of grilled shrimp.

Prep: 20 minutes **Grill:** 5 minutes (covered) or 10 minutes (uncovered) **Serves:** 6

1½ pounds fresh or frozen jumbo shrimp in shells (12 to 15)

Dressing

1 8-ounce carton plain low-fat yogurt
⅓ cup mayonnaise or salad dressing
2 tablespoons honey
1½ teaspoons curry powder
¼ teaspoon salt

Leaf lettuce
1½ cups coarsely shredded cucumber or zucchini
1½ cups coarsely shredded carrot
3 papayas, seeded, peeled, and thinly sliced
12 red or green sweet pepper rings
⅓ cup sliced almonds, toasted (optional)

1 Thaw shrimp, if frozen. Peel and devein shrimp, leaving tails intact. Rinse shrimp; pat dry with paper towels. On 6-inch skewers, thread shrimp, leaving ¼ inch between pieces. For dressing, in a small bowl stir together yogurt, mayonnaise, honey, curry powder, and salt. Cover and refrigerate until ready to serve.

2 Lightly grease the rack of an indoor electric grill or lightly coat with cooking spray. Preheat grill. Place kabobs on the grill rack. If using a covered grill, close lid. Grill until shrimp turn pink. (For a covered grill, allow 5 to 6 minutes. For an uncovered grill, allow 10 to 12 minutes, turning occasionally to cook evenly.)

3 Remove shrimp from skewers. Brush shrimp lightly with some of the dressing. Arrange lettuce on 6 dinner plates. Sprinkle cucumber and carrot over lettuce. Arrange shrimp, papaya, and sweet pepper on each salad. If desired, sprinkle with almonds. Serve the salads with the remaining dressing.

Nutrition Facts per serving: 275 cal., 12 g total fat (2 g sat. fat), 136 mg chol., 331 mg sodium, 22 g carbo., 3 g fiber, 21 g pro.
Daily Values: 104% vit. A, 142% vit. C, 15% calcium, 14% iron

food fashion

When it comes to garnishing food, follow this golden rule: keep it simple. Dress up grilled entrées with a sprig of fresh herb or a twist of citrus peel. For added flair, accent salads with ruffled kale or leaf lettuce. Add interest to foods by cutting them into eye-catching shapes. For example, bias-slice carrots or shred salad greens.

Spicy Chicken & Star Fruit ♥

It's a match made in heaven. The celestial star fruit (also called carambola) is a striking addition to this chicken dish that's a little bit Italian and a little bit Indian.

Prep: 15 minutes **Grill:** 7 minutes (covered) or 17 minutes (uncovered) **Serves:** 6

Basting Sauce

- 3 tablespoons balsamic vinegar or red wine vinegar
- 4 teaspoons olive oil
- ¾ teaspoon dried rosemary, crushed
- ½ teaspoon ground cumin
- ¼ teaspoon ground coriander
- ⅛ teaspoon black pepper
- ⅛ teaspoon ground red pepper

- 3 star fruit (carambola), sliced
- 12 green onions, cut into 2-inch pieces, and/or 4 small purple boiling onions, cut into wedges
- 6 medium skinless, boneless chicken breast halves (about 1½ pounds total)
- 3 cups hot cooked rice
- 1½ teaspoons finely shredded orange peel (optional)
- 3 tablespoons peach or apricot preserves, melted (optional)

1 For basting sauce, in a small bowl combine vinegar, olive oil, rosemary, cumin, coriander, black pepper, and red pepper. On twelve 6-inch skewers, alternately thread star fruit and onions.

2 Lightly grease the rack of an indoor electric grill or lightly coat with cooking spray. Preheat grill. Place chicken on the grill rack. If using a covered grill, close lid. Grill until chicken is tender and no longer pink. (For a covered grill, allow 4 to 6 minutes, brushing once with basting sauce the last 1 minute of grilling. For an uncovered grill, allow 12 to 15 minutes, turning and brushing once with basting sauce halfway through grilling.) Remove from grill; cover and keep warm.

3 Add kabobs to the grill rack. If using a covered grill, close lid. Grill until kabobs are heated through. (For a covered grill, allow about 3 minutes. For an uncovered grill, allow about 5 minutes, turning once halfway through grilling.) Brush kabobs with basting sauce.

4 To serve, if desired, toss rice with orange peel. Serve chicken and kabobs over rice. If desired, drizzle with preserves.

Nutrition Facts per serving: 313 cal., 5 g total fat (1 g sat. fat), 66 mg chol., 69 mg sodium, 35 g carbo., 2 g fiber, 29 g pro. Daily Values: 4% vit. A, 27% vit. C, 5% calcium, 16% iron

Filet Mignon with Portobello Sauce

Just a splash of Madeira or port wine makes this meltingly tender steak-and-mushroom dish downright marvelous. Madeira and port are both slightly sweet Spanish wines flavored with a bit of brandy.

Prep: 15 minutes **Grill:** 4 minutes (covered) or 8 minutes (uncovered) **Serves:** 6

  6 beef tenderloin steaks,
       cut 1 inch thick (about
       2 pounds total)
  2 teaspoons olive oil
  ½ teaspoon pepper
  ¼ teaspoon salt
  3 large fresh portobello
       mushrooms
 12 green onions, cut into
       1-inch pieces
  2 tablespoons margarine or
       butter
  ½ cup beef broth
  3 tablespoons Madeira or
       port wine

1 Preheat indoor electric grill. Trim fat from steaks. Rub both sides of steaks with oil and sprinkle with pepper and salt. Place steaks on the grill rack. If using a covered grill, close lid. Grill until steaks are desired doneness. (For a covered grill, allow 4 to 6 minutes for medium rare or 6 to 8 minutes for medium. For an uncovered grill, allow 8 to 12 minutes for medium rare or 12 to 15 minutes for medium, turning once halfway through grilling.)

2 Meanwhile, cut off mushroom stems even with caps; discard stems. Halve and slice mushrooms. For sauce, in a large skillet cook and stir mushrooms and green onions in hot margarine over medium heat about 5 minutes or until vegetables are tender. Stir in broth and Madeira. Bring to boiling; remove from heat. Thinly slice steaks diagonally and serve with sauce.

Nutrition Facts per serving: 476 cal., 36 g total fat (13 g sat. fat), 103 mg chol., 284 mg sodium, 5 g carbo., 3 g fiber, 30 g pro.
Daily Values: 5% vit. A, 8% vit. C, 6% calcium, 23% iron

a grill for indoors and outdoors

If your family enjoys grilling outdoors as well as in, you may want to consider one of the newest types of grills—the handy Indoor/Outdoor Grill. It looks like an ordinary outdoor unit, but the electric grill lifts off its stand so you can take it indoors. Since foods are heated from the bottom only, it performs like an uncovered indoor electric grill. It is larger than the typical indoor grill and therefore holds more food (up to 12 burgers or chops), making it ideal for entertaining. Store the grill indoors to protect the electrical components from the elements.

Stuffed Steak Pinwheels

Popeye would serve these beef pinwheels with pride. Overstuffed with spinach and smoky bacon, they are handsome to look at and especially tasty to eat.

Prep: 20 minutes **Grill:** 6 minutes (covered) or 12 minutes (uncovered) **Serves:** 6

   8 slices bacon
   1 1- to 1¼-pound beef flank steak or top round steak
  ¾ teaspoon lemon-pepper seasoning
  ¼ teaspoon salt

Filling

   1 10-ounce package frozen chopped spinach, thawed and well drained
   2 tablespoons fine dry bread crumbs
  ½ teaspoon dried thyme, crushed

1 In a large skillet cook bacon over medium heat just until brown, but not crisp. Drain on paper towels. Set aside.

2 Trim fat from steak. Score steak by making shallow diagonal cuts at 1-inch intervals in a diamond pattern. Repeat on other side. Cut steak in half lengthwise. Place a portion of steak between 2 pieces of plastic wrap. Working from the center to the edges, pound lightly with the flat side of a meat mallet into a 10×6-inch rectangle. Remove plastic wrap. Sprinkle with ¼ teaspoon of the lemon-pepper seasoning and ⅛ teaspoon of the salt. Arrange 4 bacon slices lengthwise on steak. Repeat with the remaining portion of steak.

3 Preheat indoor electric grill. For filling, in a medium bowl combine spinach, bread crumbs, thyme, and the remaining lemon-pepper seasoning. Spread half of the filling over each portion of steak. Starting from a short side, roll up each portion into a spiral. Secure with wooden toothpicks at 1-inch intervals, starting ½ inch from one end. Cutting between the toothpicks, slice each portion into six 1-inch pinwheels. On each of six 6-inch skewers, thread 2 pinwheels. Remove toothpicks.

4 Place pinwheels on the grill rack. If using a covered grill, close lid. Grill until steak is desired doneness. (For a covered grill, allow 6 to 7 minutes for medium. For an uncovered grill, allow 12 to 14 minutes for medium, turning once halfway through grilling.) To serve, remove pinwheels from skewers.

Nutrition Facts per serving: 265 cal., 15 g total fat (6 g sat. fat), 64 mg chol., 702 mg sodium, 5 g carbo., 2 g fiber, 27 g pro.
Daily Values: 36% vit. A, 16% vit. C, 7% calcium, 21% iron

Pork Satay with Tahini-Coconut Sauce

Sail with the South Sea winds—here's a sweet and lively dish that will find a port on any shore. Tahini, coconut, curry—it just keeps getting better.

Prep: 25 minutes **Marinate:** 2 hours **Grill:** 3 minutes (covered) or 10 minutes (uncovered) **Serves:** 6

1½ pounds pork tenderloin
Marinade
 ¼ cup coconut milk
 2 tablespoons lime juice
 1 tablespoon brown sugar
 1 tablespoon mild curry powder
Dipping Sauce
1½ teaspoons cooking oil
 1 tablespoon red curry paste
 ⅛ teaspoon crushed red pepper
 ¾ cup coconut milk
 ¼ cup tahini (sesame seed paste)
 4 teaspoons orange juice
 2 teaspoons brown sugar
1½ teaspoons fish sauce

1 Trim fat from meat. Cut meat into ¾-inch cubes. For marinade, in a medium bowl stir together the ¼ cup coconut milk, lime juice, the 1 tablespoon brown sugar, and curry powder. Add the meat; toss to coat. Cover and marinate in the refrigerator for 2 to 3 hours, stirring occasionally.

2 For dipping sauce, in a small saucepan heat oil over medium heat. Add curry paste and crushed red pepper; reduce heat to low. Cook and stir about 1 minute or until fragrant. Stir in the ¾ cup coconut milk, tahini, orange juice, the 2 teaspoons brown sugar, and fish sauce. Bring just to simmering. Simmer gently, uncovered, about 5 minutes or until blended and thickened, stirring frequently. Remove from heat; cover and keep warm.

3 Preheat indoor electric grill. Drain meat, discarding marinade. On 6-inch skewers, thread the meat cubes, leaving ¼ inch between pieces. Place kabobs on the grill rack. If using a covered grill, close lid.

4 Grill until meat is slightly pink in center and juices run clear. (For a covered grill, allow 3 to 5 minutes, giving kabobs a quarter turn once halfway through grilling. For an uncovered grill, allow 10 to 12 minutes, turning occasionally to cook evenly.) Serve the kabobs with dipping sauce.

Nutrition Facts per serving: 283 cal., 15 g total fat (7 g sat. fat), 81 mg chol., 223 mg sodium, 9 g carbo., 1 g fiber, 28 g pro.
Daily Values: 0% vit. A, 6% vit. C, 2% calcium, 16% iron

INDEX

Photographs indicated in **bold**.

small-grill recipes

If you're looking for a recipe that will work well on a small grill, keep these selections in mind.

Metric Cooking Hints

By making a few conversions, cooks in Australia, Canada, and the United Kingdom can use the recipes in this book with confidence. The charts on this page provide a guide for converting measurements from the U.S. customary system, which is used throughout this book, to the imperial and metric systems. There also is a conversion table for oven temperatures to accommodate the differences in oven calibrations.

Product Differences: Most of the ingredients called for in the recipes in this book are available in English-speaking countries. However, some are known by different names. Here are some common U.S. American ingredients and their possible counterparts:
- Sugar is granulated or castor sugar.
- Powdered sugar is icing sugar.
- All-purpose flour is plain household flour or white flour. When self-rising flour is used in place of all-purpose flour in a recipe that calls for leavening, omit the leavening agent (baking soda or baking powder) and salt.
- Light-colored corn syrup is golden syrup.
- Cornstarch is cornflour.
- Baking soda is bicarbonate of soda.
- Vanilla is vanilla essence.
- Green, red, or yellow sweet peppers are capsicums.
- Golden raisins are sultanas.

Volume and Weight: U.S. Americans traditionally use cup measures for liquid and solid ingredients. The following chart shows the approximate imperial and metric equivalents. If you are accustomed to weighing solid ingredients, the following approximate equivalents will help.
- 1 cup butter, castor sugar, or rice = 8 ounces = about 230 grams
- 1 cup flour = 4 ounces = about 115 grams
- 1 cup icing sugar = 5 ounces = about 140 grams

Spoon measures are used for smaller amounts of ingredients. Although the size of the tablespoon varies slightly in different countries, for practical purposes and for recipes in this book, a straight substitution is all that's necessary.

Measurements made using cups or spoons always should be level unless stated otherwise.

Equivalents: U.S. = Australia/U.K.

⅕ teaspoon = 1 ml
¼ teaspoon = 1.25 ml
½ teaspoon = 2.5 ml
1 teaspoon = 5 ml
1 tablespoon = 15 ml
1 fluid ounce = 30 ml
¼ cup = 60 ml
⅓ cup = 80 ml
½ cup = 120 ml
⅔ cup = 160 ml
¾ cup = 180 ml
1 cup = 240 ml
2 cups = 475 ml
1 quart = 1 liter
½ inch = 1.25 cm
1 inch = 2.5 cm

Baking Pan Sizes

U.S. American	Metric
8×1½-inch round baking pan	20×4-cm cake tin
9×1½-inch round baking pan	23×4-cm cake tin
11×7×1½-inch baking pan	28×18×4-cm baking tin
13×9×2-inch baking pan	32×23×5-cm baking tin
2-quart rectangular baking dish	28×18×4-cm baking tin
15×10×1-inch baking pan	38×25.5×2.5-cm baking tin (Swiss roll tin)
9-inch pie plate	22×4- or 23×4-cm pie plate
7- or 8-inch springform pan	18- or 20-cm springform or loose-bottom cake tin
9×5×3-inch loaf pan	23×13×8-cm or 2-pound narrow loaf tin or pâté tin
1½-quart casserole	1.5-liter casserole
2-quart casserole	2-liter casserole

Oven Temperature Equivalents

Fahrenheit Setting	Celsius Setting*	Gas Setting
300°F	150°C	Gas mark 2 (very low)
325°F	170°C	Gas mark 3 (low)
350°F	180°C	Gas mark 4 (moderate)
375°F	190°C	Gas mark 5 (moderately hot)
400°F	200°C	Gas mark 6 (hot)
425°F	220°C	Gas mark 7 (hot)
450°F	230°C	Gas mark 8 (very hot)
475°F	240°C	Gas mark 9 (very hot)
Broil		Grill

*Electric and gas ovens may be calibrated using Celsius. However, for an electric oven, increase the Celsius setting 10 to 20 degrees when cooking above 160°C. For convection or forced-air ovens (gas or electric), lower the temperature setting 10°C when cooking at all heat levels.